A 100-Day **Devotional** Journey
Through the Book of **Genesis**

YOUR TRUE ORIGIN STORY

MINDI WROBLEWSKI

Copyright © 2024 by Mindi Wroblewski

All rights reserved.

No portion of this book may be reproduced in any form without written permission from the publisher or author, except as permitted by U.S. copyright law.

Scripture quotations, unless otherwise noted, are taken from the Holy Bible, New International Version®, NIV®. Copyright © [2011] by Biblica, Inc.™ Used by permission. All rights reserved worldwide. The "NIV" and "New International Version" are registered trademarks of Biblica, Inc.™ Use of these trademarks requires specific permission.

Publisher
Paper Crown Media Ltd.
71-75 Shelton Street
Covent Garden
London
WC2H 9JQ
info@papercrownmedia.com
www.papercrownmedia.com

ISBN: 978-1-0685770-1-7

Cover Design: Meliza Farndell
Interior Design and Formatting: Andrea John

To my best friend and husband, Tom, whose love and support have made this journey possible.

Endorsements

Mindi Wroblewski is a woman with a heart for the things of God. Her book on Genesis is a deep draught of Biblical truth and self-examination. It's part devotional, part commentary, in which she asks straightforward, reasonable questions, identifying the foundational truths upon which any truly Biblical worldview must be based. She doesn't shy away from difficult interpretive questions, letting the Word of God be its own interpreter. If you are willing to join Mindi in her deep dive into Genesis, you will find lessons, insights, and boatloads of truth. You will also come away knowing God better than you did before.

Frank Wright, Ph.D.
Former President & Chairman, National Religious Broadcasters (NRB)

I've never known anyone more dedicated to learning and sharing the Word of God than Mindi Wroblewski. She has even memorized a good portion of Scripture. Her new book, *Your True Origin Story,* takes you on a journey through the book of Genesis much like watching a movie as you travel through the stories of our forefathers. The sequential verse summaries with commentary and historical facts are an adventure as if you are there coming along side those who lived at the time. Mindi is brilliant at connecting the events and circumstances and how they relate to our world today. The cross references provided bring deeper understanding of how and why things took place and the lessons relevant to our generation. The book is sectioned into short, easy, daily passages yet so full of knowledge and revelation. This book will be a treasure to keep, share, and read to future generations as well as an often-referenced study.

Shirley Chancellor, Author
Deactivating Triggers: Finding joy and peace in the middle of a chaotic, angry world.

Genesis is the beginning of the journey for any Christian to understand God's sovereign purpose for mankind. Through Mindi's new book, *Your True Origin Story*, she has expanded the reader's understanding of God's character and plan. By including historical evidence, personal insight, and biblical cross- referencing, Mindi invites the reader to dig deeper into the Word of God and explore how the text applies to his or her personal walk with the Lord. Whether the reader is advanced in their study of the Word of God or a new believer, this book will enrich the spiritual journey of any Christian.

Mitchell Dobrow
Mast Certified Addiction Professional
The Refuge Ranch, Program Director

The Book of Genesis is the beginning of the love letter from God to His children. In this 100-day journey of *Your True Origin Story*, my friend Mindi Wroblewski shares insight and evidence of her love for the Lord. Genesis begins with the creation story and continues through the life of Joseph. The story line includes family dynamics, stories of captivity, persecution, vengeance, love and forgiveness. Taking the time to engage in Mindi's thoughts and wisdom was a special and fulfilling enterprise for me, and I pray it will be for you as well.

Hollie Sharpe,
Insurance Claims Professional (Retired)

I love a good story--especially a true one, and Mindi Wroblewski artfully retells the ancient and well-known saga of Genesis in her *Your True Origin Story* devotional. You will come face-to-face with Almighty God and experience first-hand His love, power, and compassion as she weaves personal anecdotes with scriptural references in her distinctively personal style. This fresh look at the occurrences and characters in Genesis will leave you pondering the rich insights Mindi offers long after you finish the last page.

Georgia Schmeichel, Author
My Portion Forever

Mindi takes us on a wonderful adventure in the book of Genesis. She tosses in several other Scriptures that assist us in growing closer to PaPa (my name for our Heavenly Father). This journal will help you grow as you walk through each day with your Heavenly Father. Mindi gives us great questions to ponder, additional Scriptures to absorb, and insights into the verses at hand. All work together to give us the opportunity to stop and talk with PaPa about things we may never have thought about before. I know that Mindi's heart is to chase after the One True God as fast as her feet will run! She said "yes" and wrote this book for us to be blessed. My favorite day is the testimony of Noah, found in Genesis 6:1-8; 17. This wonderful book of the Bible is full of folks just like you and me as they walk with PaPa. The way Mindi navigates us through this adventure is fun and powerful at the same time. You will be blessed as you walk through the next 100 days with my friend, Mindi.

Leigh Ann Pearson, Author
Bulverde, Texas

Mindi's deep study of the book of Genesis has resulted in a pleasant and readable blend of theological truth combined with practical principles for Christian living. The result is a journey through the lives and times of early biblical characters, those long-ago people whose lives have plenty of relevance and application for us today.

Jeff Michaels,
Teacher at Lighthouse Christian School

Acknowledgements

This book could not have been written without the help of others: I appreciate each one who took the time to read through and then write an endorsement. I know it was a time-consuming endeavor, and there aren't enough words to express my gratitude. My professional editor, Ava Pennington, not only made me a better writer but was eloquent and even humorous in her rebuke of my sometimes long-sentences, idioms, and theology. I feel more confident than ever about what is written on these pages because of her. Meliza Farndell, whose God-given gifts have blessed and encouraged many, not only designed the cover page for *Your True Origin Story* but was instrumental in coming up with the title! She has an amazing ability to touch the heart of authors, and I am excited about her new publishing adventure Paper Crown Media that is publishing my book. I am also thankful for Andrea John, whose skill in formatting made it possible to complete all that goes into writing and publishing a book. Thank you to my family and friends whose support and love gave me the encouragement I needed to complete this project.

From the Song "Ancient Words"
By Michael W. Smith

Holy Words long preserved
For our walk in this world
They resound with God's own heart
O let the ancient words impart
Words of life, words of hope
Give us strength, help us cope
In this world where'er we roam
Ancient words will guide us home.

The Lord merely spoke,
and the heavens were created.
He breathed the word,
and all the stars were born.
He assigned the sea its boundaries
and locked the oceans in vast reservoirs.
Let the whole world fear the Lord,
and let everyone stand in awe of him.
For when he spoke, the world began!
It appeared at his command.

Psalm 33:6-9

Introduction

When people write books, the words on each page have meaning and purpose. Every chapter tells the story, whether fiction, nonfiction, instruction, or teaching on the issue being written about. There's a beginning, middle, and end. This is also true of the Bible, except this is a compilation of inspired books telling us God's story. When read from this perspective, the Bible can do amazing things for us. We discover who we are, why we are here, and what we are meant to do with our lives as we learn who is behind this crazy thing called life. The wonderful truth is, God is not crazy, but life without Him is.

We are often so busy we may not have a lot of time to sit and read large passages of the Bible. This is why each day I have included a reference to short sections from Genesis by chapter and verse. It will give you the opportunity to open your own Bible and read the version that speaks the most to you.

I love reading devotional books. They are short, yet inspirational, and provide a way to spend time with the Lord. *Your True Origin Story* takes you through the entire book of Genesis. It's a story like none other because it is God's story, and His story includes you! Meet the people who came before you. Learn about their real-life struggles and how their encounters with God carved the way for us to find Jesus, the Savior.

I have learned much about our heavenly Father through this entire process, and I am excited to share what I've learned with others. I'm no scholar, teacher, or philosopher, but I do have a heart for Jesus and a desire to know Him better. We do this by reading what is written in His profound book that teaches us not only who we are but who God wants us to be, and who we can become in Him.

I grew up in a tumultuous family atmosphere. The oldest of six, as each subsequent brother was born, I found myself feeling increasingly isolated, especially in the shadow of my locally-famous father who played defensive end for the San Francisco 49ers until I was thirteen years old. When my sister was born, I was fifteen and had already entered the age of rebellion against authority. My parents and even my friends tried to reign in my sometimes erratic behavior. If it wasn't for our grandma, who lived with us, I probably wouldn't be alive today. It makes me heartsick to think of the hurt and disrespect that at times spewed out of my mouth, while I felt totally justified with such behavior. This is who I was, but it is no longer who I am, which is why I love sharing God's story with others.

We all have struggles; no two the same, yet, we all have similar questions about life such as: *Who am I? Why am I here? Is this all there is to life? What happens when I die?*

My prayer is that as we go through the book of Genesis, those questions will be answered in a way that opens your heart, soul, mind, and spirit to the one, true God who not only gave you your identity but who knows you from the inside out. His greatest desire is for you to know Him and desire an intimate relationship that will change the direction of your life. This relationship will give you hope not only for the future but for every day. You are so loved! Isn't it amazing the Creator of all things wants to have a relationship with you, and me?

Sit back, relax, and enjoy the journey. I pray it will transform your life, as it has mine.

Day 1

In the Beginning

Genesis 1:1-5

"Before the mountains were born or you brought forth the whole world, from everlasting to everlasting you are God" (Psalm 90:2). This is a difficult concept to grasp—that before God spoke the world into existence, He was—but I believe it. Why? Because of the gift of faith, without which "it is impossible to please God" (Hebrews 11:6).

A young pastor I know once asked the question, "If you believe what you say you believe about Jesus, shouldn't it be easy to defend your faith?" Then he said something that astonished me: a majority of Christians he knew do not read the Bible on a regular basis, especially the Old Testament. If that's true, and I have no reason to doubt him, could that be the reason so many Christians remain silent about their faith?

What about you? How often do you read the Bible? Have you ever read it one time through?

If you read it on a regular basis beginning with Genesis, questions such as where you came from are answered. Science tells us we morphed into humans from apes over millions of years. If so, how did it happen? Did scientists witness it, write it down, and can they say with 100 percent certainty this is the way life came about? It takes a lot of faith to believe that, doesn't it?

Nothing is created from nothing. Mark Lowry, a gospel singer and comedian, once gave an example that stuck with me. He said, "Order never comes from chaos, unless somebody puts it together. You know, if I took my watch apart... and stuffed the pieces in a sack, and then I shook the sack for six billion years, what if after six billion years--what would be the chances of me pulling out a watch that is ticking and on time? I don't even have enough faith for that." His point being, those parts didn't magically come together to make a working watch. Someone with expertise and knowledge had to take each piece and put it in its proper place before it could function as intended.[1]

And such is life. There had to be someone or something behind creation, just as with anything else such as electricity, airplanes, cars, buildings, washing machines, and human beings. The list is endless. There *is* Someone who gives witness to this. It all begins in Genesis and continues through the entire Bible. This is not a scientific book, determining the method of how and when things happened, but it is a revelation of how we got here, how we should live while we are here, and where we are going.

Open the Bible and the first three words are: "In the beginning." But it is the words that follow this unique opening that reveal the beginning to which they refer: "God created the heavens and the earth. Now the earth was formless and empty, darkness was over the surface of the deep, and the Spirit of God was hovering over the waters" (Genesis 1:1-2). This is where it all began. Believe this and you will have a firm foundation upon which to believe the rest of the Bible.

We are also told in John 1:1-3, "In the beginning was the Word, and the Word was with God, and the Word was God. He was with God in the beginning. Through him all things were made; without him nothing was made that has been made." Then, when God spoke, out of the darkness came light.

If you have ever been on a cave tour, you know what it's like when the guide turns off the light. It is so dark you can't even see your hand in front of your face. It is an eerie feeling that can bring gripping fear. Then when the light comes on, you can see the person next to you; the walls slowly become visible, and even the ripples in the water bring comfort. God knows we need the light to survive, not only physically but spiritually.

As we open our hearts to God's word from the very beginning of time, let's look to Him to guide us through the darkness by His glorious light. We will begin to see things as never before when we lean into Him, for His truth is the light that brings us out of darkness (2 Corinthians 4:6).

Heavenly Father, as we begin this journey into Genesis, impart Your wisdom and understanding. Open my heart to the revelation of Your Word, which gives answers to where I came from, who I am, why I am here, and where I am going. I want to know You intimately. In Jesus' name, I pray. Amen.

Day 2

Separation

Genesis 1:6-8

When God spoke, things happened. By His words, an expanse called the "sky" was created to separate the waters above and below it. Can you envision the power it took for this to happen? Even a bomb as powerful as the one dropped on Japan at the end of WWII couldn't produce such a feat.

We are only in Day 2 and if you are not yet getting the majesty and might of the Creator, don't despair. There's much more to come.

When God separated the waters, the sky appeared. We all know what the sky is. All we have to do is tilt our heads upward to see it. And every day we see water on earth in one form or another. This is the water we can see, touch and drink. It sustains us and is necessary for our physical wellbeing. But there is also a living water to which Jesus referred, one which is necessary for our spiritual wellbeing (John 4:14).

Jesus gave us insight into this living water when He spoke with a Samaritan woman who came to draw from Jacob's well. When Jesus saw her, He asked, "Will you give me a drink?" (John 4:7). She was taken aback by his request as Jews did not talk to Samaritans, especially women. But He answered her by saying, "If you knew the gift of God and who it is that asks you for a drink, you would have asked him and he would have given you living water" (John 4:10).

Astonished at His response, she said, "Sir, you have nothing to draw with and the well is deep. Where can you get this living water?" (John 4:11)

Jesus answered, "Everyone who drinks this water [from the well] will be thirsty again, but whoever drinks the water I give them will never thirst. Indeed, the water

I give them will become in them a spring of water welling up to eternal life" (John 4:13-14).

Though the water on earth satisfies us for a time, the living water to which Jesus referred sustains us into eternity. Jesus explained it this way: "'Let anyone who is thirsty come to me and drink. Whoever believes in me, as Scripture has said, rivers of living water will flow from within them.' By this he meant the Spirit, whom those who believed in him were later to receive" (John 7:37-39). Jesus was not only referring to His disciples, but also to those who would come after them (Acts 2:38-39). What an incredible gift this is!

Lord, thank You that I can rest in the knowledge that You are my Creator and You know everything about me, my needs, my wants, and my desires. You have the answers to my questions and You desire me to know You in an intimate way. Draw me into Your presence as I journey through Your Word from the very beginning of time. In Jesus' name, I pray. Amen.

Day 3
God's Invisible Qualities

Genesis 1:9-13

Psalm 29:3-9 proclaims, "The voice of the Lord is over the waters; the God of glory thunders, the Lord thunders over the mighty waters. The voice of the Lord is powerful; the voice of the Lord is majestic. The voice of the Lord breaks the cedars; the Lord breaks in pieces the cedars of Lebanon[1]".

When God spoke and the land and sea separated, "His voice was like the roar of rushing waters, and the land was radiant with his glory" (Ezekiel 43:2). The sound must have been deafening, more powerful than the roar of Niagra Falls[2].

The majesty of God's presence on the earth produced not only land but mountains and valleys, canyons and caves; waterfalls streaming down mountainsides into creeks and rivers. The beauty and grandeur of it all would have been breathtaking. When God finished, He saw that it was good and, as a once popular song proclaimed, "We've only just begun."[3]

"Then God said, 'Let the land produce vegetation: seed-bearing plants and trees on the land that bear fruit with seed in it, according to their various kinds.' And it was so" (Genesis 1:11). The plants, flowers, trees, and vegetables that exist would take more than a person's lifetime to know them all.

Not only did God create them, but each one has within it seed for reproducing. It wasn't a one-time event but it was meant to be perpetual. God prepared the earth to be inhabited. He knew what was needed, and He saw that it was good.

If we want to know who our heavenly Father is, all we have to do is look around us and we will see His creation. The earth remains with its land and seas. "God's invisible qualities—his eternal power and divine nature—have been clearly seen, being understood from what has been made, so that people are without excuse" (Romans 1:20).

There is a book that tells us what we need to know without spending a lifetime trying to figure it out on our own. Don't wait until you step into eternity to meet "the Judge of all" (Hebrews 12:23) when you can know Him now.

God is real. He is mighty. He is all-knowing and all-powerful. There is no one like Him. Apart from Him, there is no God (Isaiah 44:24; 45:6).

Lord, thank You for the simplicity with which You have revealed Your creation. Thank You that I don't need a dissertation or multi-page explanation as to how it all began. Help me receive what You have so freely given. In Jesus' name, I pray. Amen.

Day 4

The Sun, Moon, and Stars

Genesis 1:14-19

When God made the sun, the moon, and the stars, He said they were set in the sky to separate the light from the darkness. They were signs to mark the seasons, days and years.

Since that fourth day of creation, there have been many books written about the sun, the moon, and the stars, and how they affect life on earth. Some make a livelihood by saying they can read the lines on a person's palm or gaze into a crystal ball and predict the future. These psychics and fortune tellers create elaborate charts that go into great detail about what will happen in a person's future based solely on the placement of the sun, moon, stars, and planets when a person was born. We are told in Scripture to avoid consulting with such people (Leviticus 19:31).

They certainly don't provide this potentially life-altering information for free. They take what God spoke into existence and use it for their own selfish, sometimes evil, purposes. But why pay someone to chart your future or gaze into a crystal ball when you can know the One who "merely spoke, and the heavens were created. He breathed the word, and all the stars were born" (Psalm 33:6 NLT)

In Job's book, he says, "He [God] covers the face of the full moon, spreading his clouds over it. (Job 26:9).

Paul wrote to the Corinthians: "The sun has one kind of splendor, the moon another and the stars another; and star differs from star in splendor" (1 Corinthians 15:41). And Psalm 96:5-6 tells us, "For all the gods of the nations are idols, but the Lord made the heavens. Splendor and majesty are before him; strength and glory are in his sanctuary."

There is no reason to worry about the things we don't fully understand. We know the One who created everything, and He tells us: "Do not be anxious about anything, but in every situation, by prayer and petition, with thanksgiving, present your requests to God. And the peace of God, which transcends all understanding, will guard your hearts and your minds in Christ Jesus" (Philippians 4:6-7).

Lord, may the eyes of my heart be enlightened that I may know the hope to which You have called me, the riches of Your glorious inheritance in the saints, and Your incomparably great power to those who believe (Ephesians 1:18). In Jesus' name, I pray. Amen.

Day 5

Oceans and Birds

Genesis 1:20-23

What is hidden below the surface of the waters is so different from what exists on earth, it's not easy to understand how the creatures of the sea survive. When I was a kid, I loved watching Jacques Cousteau on television as he explored the mysteries below the ocean surface. He spent his life researching and studying the creatures of the sea. He used divers with cameras to capture photos of whales, sharks, eels, and so much more to share with the world, but he couldn't even come close to capturing it all.

According to the Science News[1] website, "In a new study, scientists amassed and analyzed more than 100,000 published records of animals found in the Clarion-Clipperton Zone [central and eastern Pacific Ocean] with some records dating back to the 1870s. About 90 percent of species from these records were previously undescribed: There were only about 440 named species compared with roughly 5,100 without scientific names." Ninety percent undescribed means there's a long way to go before discovering and naming all of them!

Where did all of these living things that swim the waters of earth come from? We need look no further than Genesis 1:20.

In addition to the sea life, there are the different species and subspecies of birds. They come in all shapes, sizes, and colors. Some can fly, some cannot. According to multiple websites, there are 9,000 to 10,000 species of birds in the world, maybe even double that. It would take more than a few scientists to learn the intricate details of each species.

In Psalm 24:1-2, King David proclaimed, "The earth is the Lord's, and everything in it, the world, and all who live in it; for he founded it on the seas and established it on the waters." If we believe this, we can enjoy all He created on earth, into eternity, where He tells us, "What no eye has seen, what no ear has heard, and what no human mind has conceived--the things God has prepared for those who love him" (1 Corinthians 2:9).

Psalm 148:7, 10, and 13 proclaim: "Praise the Lord from the earth, you great sea creatures and all ocean depths . . . wild animals and all cattle, small creatures and flying birds . . . praise the name of the Lord, for his name alone is exalted; his splendor is above the earth and the heavens."

Lord, what was it like to create these glorious things in the earth? Were You singing as You created? Were You shouting with joy? Were You laughing with excitement? May I be so bold as to ask that You bring me into Your mighty presence, reveal to me Your glory and the magnificence of who You are, my Creator, my Lord and my King. In Jesus' name, I pray. Amen.

Day 6

Creation Continues

Genesis 1:24-31

Wow! A lot happened on the sixth day, which culminated with a clear instruction from God that He was putting man and woman in charge of all His creation. In our world today, that notion has been turned upside down. Animals, trees, plants, even food have come to the forefront of our priorities, so much so that some people make them more important than their fellow human beings. But it was for human beings that all of these things were created; not the other way around.

Perhaps it's because we are so far removed from when God created us that we are making up our own rules to live by. But that's like a child, who has no life experience, saying to their parents, "I don't have to do anything you say because I already know everything, and you don't know anything!" That would not go over very well in most families, would it?

By delving into what God said, we can gain a greater appreciation and understanding of how life is intended to be lived. "But blessed is the one who trusts in the Lord, whose confidence is in him" (Jeremiah 17:7). We can trust Him because He is God (Psalm 3:5-8), and He was there before the very beginning. If we listen, He will teach us what we need to know about this wonderful thing called life.

Lord, help me trust in You with all of my heart and lean not on my own understanding. In all of my ways help me to acknowledge You, knowing You will make my paths straight (Proverbs 3:6). In Jesus' name, I pray. Amen.

Day 7

No God but God

Re-read Genesis 1

More than likely, Moses was one of the most highly educated people of his time, having been raised in a king's palace by Pharaoh's daughter (Exodus 2:10). He was probably taught by the most brilliant minds who were available at Pharaoh's beck and call. Why is this important to know? It is my understanding, from extensive research, that Moses is the author of Genesis.

One source to delve more fully into this is an article written by Bodie Hodge and Dr. Terry Mortensen titled *Did Moses Write Genesis?*[1]

You might say, "But Moses wasn't there. How could he know all of this?" This, too is backed up by many scriptures quoted in the above article[2]. The statement in their article, which sums up their conclusions, says: "It is easy to deny Mosaic authorship, if one ignores the evidence for it. But that is not honest scholarship."

My conclusion from their research: Moses wrote not only Genesis but the succeeding four books, known as the Pentateuch[3]. Not only were these events handed down from generation to generation, but God was there. These are things no one but God could know. I believe He inspired Moses to write them down so we can know Him and know the truth of how it all began.

This may lead to another question, such as: "How do we know it happened this way if no human was there?" Isaiah 46:9-11 tells us, "Remember the former things, those of long ago; I am God, and there is no other; I am God, and there is none like me. I make known the end from the beginning, from ancient times, what is still to come…What I have said, that will I bring about; what I have planned, that I will do." If there is no other God but God and He cannot lie

(Hebrews 6:18); if He always existed, then He was there and He alone can testify that what He made actually happened, and that it was good.

There are some who might ask, "How could God have always existed?" This can be a little confusing, even resulting in circular thinking that has no end, but there is a way to find out. In a court of law, there is something called "circumstantial evidence," which means you can conclude certain facts by the circumstances. The book of Genesis tells us in the beginning God was there, and in the book of Revelation, the last book of the Bible, Jesus confirms this when He says, "I am the Alpha [the beginning] and the Omega [the end], who is, and who was, and who is to come, the Almighty" (Revelation 1:8). This is the circumstantial evidence which can lead us to conclude that God was, is, and always will be. From the beginning to the end, He was and is there.

We can debate this until our dying breath, but "What good will it be for someone to gain the whole world, yet forfeit their soul? Or what can anyone give in exchange for their soul?" (Matthew 16:26). The answer is: nothing. All the answers we need for life are contained in the Bible.

"And without faith it is impossible to please God, because anyone who comes to him must believe that he exists and that he rewards those who earnestly seek him" (Hebrews 11:6). All we are asked to do is receive what God says, believe what He not only says but what He has done, trust Him, and then live by faith. Jesus, our Lord and Savior, has done the rest (Ephesians 1:11-14).

Lord, may my heart take delight in knowing You are the one true God and what You say You will do. I can count on it! In Jesus' name, I pray. Amen.

Day 8

A Day of Rest

Genesis 2:1-2

Does anyone today know what it means to really rest? God did. In six days, He created the earth with waters, lands, mountains, valleys, birds, sea creatures, cattle, creatures that move along the ground, and wild animals according to their various kinds. He laid the foundation that would enable the man and woman He created to live in His perfect world and take care of it all.

God did not need a physical rest because He was exhausted, but because He finished what He began and it was time to stop His work (Hebrews 4:3-4). How often do we do that, if at all? I know I am guilty of being constantly on the go. Even as a Christian, there was a time when I rarely rested. I didn't even attend church very often on Sundays because I had other things to do. I justified my behavior, but deep down I knew I was not pleasing the Lord.

Even if we don't read the Bible, we know we need rest. Turn on the television, read the paper, go on the internet, you can get exhausted searching for places to find rest and relaxation. Even planning a short vacation for a few days can bring with it a tension that takes away the pleasure of "getting away." But God blessed the seventh day and made it a holy day for rest (Genesis 2:3), and that has never changed.

When Sunday comes this week, take the day to consider what God meant to rest and keep the day holy. Let Him speak to your heart, and He will make it clear how He wants you to accomplish this at the end of a busy six days' work. "For anyone who enters God's rest also rests from their works, just as God did from his" (Hebrews 4:10).

Lord, I honestly don't know what it means to rest. The pressures of life at times overwhelm me and my mind races a million miles an hour. Help me, Father, to enter Your rest so I can find renewal and refreshment for my body, mind, soul, and spirit. In Jesus' name, I pray. Amen.

Day 9

A Day of Rest Continues

Genesis 2:3

Before we get into why rest is important, think of someone famous, someone whose life had a major impact on others. Henry Ford comes to my mind. He manufactured and produced cars so that not only the rich but the average person could afford this luxury. Ford implemented the gift God gave him, and not many people would question his knowledge and authority when it came to cars because he was there from the very beginning.

Yet, when we read what God said about creation, the One who not only witnessed all that took place but caused it all to happen, we have no problem questioning what He tells us. We will soon discover why this is, but for now let's go back to God's creation which took place over the course of seven days, what we know as a week.

More than 6,000 years later, seven days remains a time marker for one week. When God finished all He had created in six days, when He saw that it was all good, He set apart the seventh day and made it holy. If the Creator of the world thought it was necessary to rest after all His work, why should we think any differently?

In the not-too-distant past in America, Sunday was set aside as a day of worship and prayer, a day to spend with family enjoying each other's company and talking about all the week's activities. Today, it is just another day for many people. There used to be Blue Laws which required businesses to close, allowing families an opportunity to attend church, and also rest. This has changed so drastically that now society considers it almost weird that places like Hobby Lobby and Chick-fil-A close their doors on Sunday.

Not only do professional sports vie with family and church time on Sunday, but the kids are bombarded with choices in sports such as soccer, football, and basketball. These activities often require travel away from home on the weekends.

When we weigh our options in today's culture, this might be a good teaching opportunity for our kids to show them what is important in our lives and how to balance our commitment to God with the pressures of this world.

The Sabbath day was so important to the Lord, He included it in the Ten Commandments: "Remember the Sabbath day by keeping it holy" (Exodus 20:8). Have we gotten so far away from God that we have forgotten the Sabbath day to keep it holy?

"Therefore tell the people: This is what the Lord Almighty says: 'Return to me,' declares the Lord Almighty, 'and I will return to you,' says the Lord Almighty" (Zechariah 1:3). It's time we go back to the things that really matter by putting God first in our lives. That includes honoring Him with a day of rest.

Lord, fill my heart with Your presence. Guide me by Your Spirit and give me the ability to be in tune with Your plans and purposes for my life, including taking the time needed to stop working and rest. In Jesus' name, I pray. Amen.

Day 10

Adam and Eve

Genesis 2:4-25

People-watching is one of my favorite pastimes, and shopping at Walmart is a reminder of how diverse and creative the Lord is. There are young, old, tall, short, fat, thin, long-haired, short-haired, bald, and people of various skin colors. We are different, yet the same. We all have one head, one nose, one mouth, two ears, two eyes, a neck, a chest, a body, two arms, two hands, two legs, and two feet. We are told in Psalm 100:3, "Know that the Lord is God. It is he who made us, and we are his; we are his people, the sheep of his pasture." If we stop and contemplate this, it truly is amazing.

After the Lord created Adam, He put him in the garden of Eden to work it and take care of it. But there was a slight problem: "The Lord God said, 'It is not good for the man to be alone. I will make a helper suitable for him'" (Genesis 2:18). Then something happened which is greatly debated in our modern world. "So the Lord God caused the man to fall into a deep sleep; and while he was sleeping, he took one of the man's ribs and then closed up the place with flesh. Then the Lord God made a woman from the rib he had taken out of the man, and he brought her to the man" (Genesis 2:21-22).

Notice that God says "helper," not servant, not slave, not unequal, but "helper." Today, the lines are blurred to the point where some people question whether they are even a man or woman. This may seem sane to some but, in reality, believing we are the master of our own destiny and we can be whatever it is we want to be causes a lot of confusion. It takes away from who and what God created us to be: a man or a woman.

In the book of the prophet Jeremiah, God says, "Before I formed you in the womb I knew you, before you were born I set you apart; I appointed you as a prophet to the nations" (Jeremiah 1:5). This was not only a word for Jeremiah but it is a word for us. God does not make mistakes. He knew us before we were formed in the womb and He set us apart to be a holy people for Him (Ephesians 1:4). Though we may not be appointed a prophet to the nations, He knows the plans He has for us, plans to prosper and not to harm, plans to give hope and a future (Jeremiah 29:11).

God knew the plans He had for Adam and Eve. He knew what was best for them, but the choice was theirs. Would they remain perfect before the Lord and follow His plan or would they choose to go their own way apart from Him? Sadly, we know the answer.

Oh, but the story has not yet ended. It is only beginning, and we are about to embark on a journey that will make it possible to know the God who spoke and it came to pass; the God who loves us with an everlasting love and draws us to Him with loving kindness. He is the Lord, the God of all creation. Is there anything too hard for Him? (Isaiah 14:27; 43:13; Jeremiah 32:27).

Lord, Your creation is beyond my understanding. The design and workings of the human body are a magnificent testimony to Your greatness. Help me remember I did not form myself but it was You who chose to make me in Your image, to Your glory and honor. It is me who chooses to go my own way. When I do, Lord, bring me back to You that I may know You intimately once again. In Jesus' name, I pray. Amen.

Day 11

The Fall of Humanity

Genesis 3:1-6

"Now the serpent was more crafty than any of the wild animals the Lord God had made." Apparently, the serpent could speak and Eve was close enough to hear him when he asked, "Did God really say, 'You must not eat from any tree in the garden'?" Eve responded to the serpent, "We may eat fruit from the trees in the garden, but God did say, 'You must not eat fruit from the tree that is in the middle of the garden, and you must not touch it, or you will die'" (Genesis 3:1-3).

Then, like the sly devil we know him to be, I imagine him in a snarly, sort of "I know it all" way, saying, "You will not certainly die. For God knows that when you eat from it your eyes will be opened, and you will be like God, knowing good and evil" (Genesis 3:4-5). In other words, "Who does God think He is? You can decide for yourself what is good and what is evil."

Was God testing them? Maybe. But it was also a matter of who was in the better position to determine the consequences of knowing the difference between good and evil; God, the Creator, or man, the created? Think of your own children. When you bring them into this world, they are tiny and vulnerable, and need protection. Who better to make decisions on their behalf than you? Soon, though, they want to do things themselves and you find yourself saying, "Don't touch the stove," or "Keep away from the knives." They are too young to understand why, but if they disobey it doesn't take long to figure out that stoves burn and knives cut! It's too late then. They've done it their own way and will have to suffer the consequences, just like Adam and Eve did when they decided they knew better than God. They really didn't, but the damage was done, and they had to face the consequences; consequences we still live under to this day.

The serpent's remarks must have sounded pretty plausible. The Bible doesn't tell us this, but my thought is Eve had likely been hanging around listening to the serpent for a while and convinced herself that what he was telling her was true. This time when she looked at the fruit of the tree, it appeared good for food and pleasing to the eye. Because she now believed it was desirable for gaining wisdom, she took and ate it. Not wanting to be alone in this delectable taste of fruit, she handed it to her husband, who also ate it.

Why was there craftiness in God's perfect creation? Was it to see if Adam and Eve would remain faithful, or believe the lie of the serpent? Was it because of the earlier rebellion in the heavenly realms (Isaiah 14:12-14)? I do not know, but I do know "God is faithful; he will not let you be tempted beyond what you can bear. But when you are tempted, he will also provide a way out so that you can endure it" (1 Corinthians 10:13). "When tempted, no one should say, 'God is tempting me.' For God cannot be tempted by evil, nor does he tempt anyone; but each person is tempted when they are dragged away by their own evil desire and enticed. Then, after desire has conceived, it gives birth to sin; and sin when it is full-grown, gives birth to death" (James 1:13-15).

Eve allowed her desire to become full-grown and she gave into her temptation, which eventually did lead to death. May we learn from this that sin has severe consequences and let us persevere under trial, so that when we have stood the test, we will receive the crown of life that the Lord has promised to those who love him (James 1:12).

Heavenly Father, may my prayer be as Jesus taught us to pray: Do not let us yield to temptation but deliver us from evil. In Jesus' name, I pray. Amen.

Day 12

The Confrontation

Genesis 3:7-15

It wasn't long after Eve and Adam ate the forbidden fruit that God came to the garden in the cool of the day and called out to them.

They did not answer.

Do you think God was surprised they were hiding from Him? No, He wasn't surprised, and He isn't surprised when we try and hide after doing something wrong.

But why do we want to hide? Shame? Guilt? Don't want to own up to it? Whatever the reason, it is impossible to hide from God. "Nothing in all creation is hidden from God's sight. Everything is uncovered and laid bare before the eyes of him to whom we must give account" (Hebrews 4:13).

The Lord called out to Adam, "Where are you?"

Adam answered, "I heard you in the garden, and I was afraid because I was naked; so I hid."

God responded by asking, "Who told you that you were naked? Have you eaten from the tree that I commanded you not to eat from?"

Adam shows no humility or remorse for his actions and actually blames "The woman you put here with me—she gave me some fruit from the tree, and I ate it" (Genesis 3:9-12).

If you read Adam's words carefully, he not only blamed Eve but he also blamed God!

We sometimes have the same attitude. We blame others for our shortcomings and problems rather than take responsibility for our actions and admit our failures. I'll admit, I'm guilty of such things. How about you?

The Lord turned to Eve and asked, "What is this you have done?"

She responded similarly by blaming "the serpent deceived me, and I ate" (Genesis 3:13). She certainly was a quick learner.

The Lord then cursed the serpent above all the livestock and wild animals, adding, "You will crawl on your belly and you will eat dust all the days of your life" (Genesis 3:14).

That one act of disobedience changed the entire course of human history. Thankfully, God was not unprepared for this. He had a plan.

I sometimes wonder if Adam and Eve had only been humble and contrite, coming before the Lord in repentance and asking forgiveness, would He have given them a second chance? We will never know because the moment rebellion set in, it gained a stronghold that would not be broken until Jesus came to set the captive free (Luke 4:18-19).

Lord, I am only beginning to understand Your unfolding story of creation, rebellion, forgiveness, and redemption. Open my eyes to see and my ears to hear as You show me what is good and what is pleasing in Your sight. In Jesus' name, I pray. Amen.

Day 13

The Curse

Genesis 3:16-24

The seriousness of sin can be summed up in one word: death. Why? Because God, who is holy, will not look upon nor tolerate sin (Habakkuk 1:13), yet, He is compassionate and loving (Lamentations 3:22-23).

If you are a parent, you have experienced one of the closest things to God's love on this earth. You hold in your arms a bearer of your own image, who at that very moment seems pure and innocent. They grow up all too quickly, and can soon be demanding; even rebellious, deliberately disregarding any instructions you might give them. When this happens, do you stop loving them? Do you want to harm them? Would you go so far as to kill them? Of course, not!

Consider then that God, in His mercy, who was full of love for His creation, did not want to harm or kill Adam and Eve the moment they sinned against Him. There were grave consequences to their sin, though, something which many might consider a ruthless act, but one which was necessary to demonstrate the seriousness of defying God's command.

Their makeshift clothing of fig leaves was inadequate to cover their shame. It would take much more. Someone or something had to die. God chose to kill an animal or animals, then use the skins to cover their nakedness. The Bible does not explicitly say this, but most likely what was covered were the private parts of the body. Why do you think that is? I believe it would take more than a day's devotional to delve into this, so I won't. What is important is for the first time since God proclaimed everything He created was good, blood was shed for their sin that was very bad, which is a recurring theme throughout all of Scripture.

Adam and Eve must have contemplated eating from the tree of life situated in the middle of Eden, but God was not about to let that happen. He escorted them out of Eden; then placed a cherubim and a flaming sword flashing back and forth on the east side of the garden so they couldn't get anywhere near the tree of life. He was not going to allow them to live forever in their sin. Alleluia to that!

Since that sorrowful day, life has never been easy. Now Adam had to work by the sweat of his brow to grow food. Eve would experience great pain as she brought their children into the world. And it wouldn't be long before their two sons, Cain and Abel, grew up and the first recorded murder took place. When sin entered the world, the genie was let out of the bottle, and there was no way to put it back; and this genie didn't grant three wishes. It only brought with it rebellion, deceit, and unbelief, the world in which we live today.

Lord, it's a mystery how Adam and Eve believed You lied to them. But when I consider the world in which we live today, things haven't changed. There seems to be more unbelief than ever. Thank You for sending Jesus to take away my sins and bring me back into a relationship with You. Thank You for the hope this brings not only for now but for the future. In Jesus' name, I pray. Amen.

Day 14

Cain and Abel

Genesis 4:1-7

Sadly, throughout my life, I have too often been quick to dish out criticism. When it comes to receiving it, my quickness disappears like a turtle hiding its head in its shell. I don't like being on the receiving end. However, criticism can be a good thing when it's meant to help someone be right with God. "Do not rebuke mockers or they will hate you; rebuke the wise and they will love you. Instruct the wise and they will be wiser still; teach the righteous and they will add to their learning" (Proverbs 9:8-9). Jesus said, "Those whom I love I rebuke and discipline. So be earnest and repent" (Revelation 3:19), which brings us to today's message.

Adam and Eve had two sons. The oldest was named Cain; the youngest, Abel. There came a time that "By faith Abel brought God a better offering than Cain did. By faith, he [Abel] was commended as righteous, when God spoke well of his offerings" (Hebrews 11:4). This made Cain very angry.

"Then the Lord said to Cain, 'Why are you angry? Why is your face downcast? If you do what is right, will you not be accepted? But if you do not do what is right, sin is crouching at your door; it desires to have you, but you must rule over it'" (Genesis 4:6-7). Isn't the Lord gracious and kind, even gentle in His criticism? He is asking Cain to think about what he has done and consider the consequences. The choice was his.

How do we measure up in the choices we make each day? Are we trying to do things our way, like Cain, to show how great we are, or are we like Abel, who exemplified "sincerity of heart and reverence for the Lord" (Colossians 3:22)?

It's not easy to search our hearts, is it? But it is necessary because the Lord is watching. He judges the thoughts and attitudes of the heart (Hebrews 4:12).

Lord, many times I have fallen short of what I know pleases You. I act and speak before I think and do not always consider others. Help me listen when You speak, learn from what You say and, most importantly, do what You require. In Jesus' name, I pray. Amen.

Day 15

Anger

Genesis 4:8

Anger is a powerful emotion. If left unchecked, it begins to fester like an open wound, until suddenly, like a volcano, it explodes and everything within spews forth. It leaves a path of destruction and devastation. Unlike a volcano, though, anger can be controlled if it is pulled up by its roots to wither and die like a weed. This was the choice Cain faced. But like his father before him, he refused God's warning. As a result, he murdered his brother, whom he should have protected and loved.

The innocent, the one who had done nothing wrong, suffered at the hand of the guilty, which is another recurrent theme throughout the Bible. Cain set a standard for wickedness, and though anger may not always result in murder, it can destroy the very heart and soul of all who are its target. That's not all. When its owner refuses to release anger, pride and arrogance compound grief.

After Abel's murder, the Lord asked Cain, "Where is your brother Abel?" Every time I read this response, I cringe at the thought of answering God Almighty this way, but there it is in black and white. "I don't know," Cain replied. "Am I my brother's keeper?" (Genesis 4:9).

When confronted with his crime by the God who knows all things, Cain refused to yield. It was as though the anger he felt had seeped deep into his very being to the point that no matter what God said to him, he could not or would not take responsibility for his own actions (Proverbs 29:11).

What about you? Do you allow God to search your heart, mind, and soul? If so, what is your response when He reveals the truth of your innermost thoughts and desires? Do you become angry or do you confess your sin and master it (1 John 1:8-11)? The choice has eternal consequences.

Lord, forgive me for the times I have allowed anger to well up within me and destroy not only my peace but the peace of those around me. Search my heart, my mind, my soul, and see if there is any evil thought or desire within me. Help me be honest with You and with myself, for I know You have given me the strength and power to overcome. In Jesus' name, I pray. Amen.

Day 16

The Punishment

Genesis 4:9-24

For almost fifteen years, I worked in the federal court system. I witnessed many defendants take the stand to try and convince a jury that they were innocent of the crimes for which they were charged. I've even heard one or two admit their guilt, yet try and finagle their way out by justifying what they did. What struck me most was their lack of shame or remorse. Their only concern was to somehow get away with their crime and avoid punishment.

It's not the first time this has happened; nor will it be the last. It happened with Adam and Eve, and again in Genesis 4 when God confronted Cain with the murder of his brother, then pronounced judgment on him. Cain's only concern was that his punishment was more than he could bear. Without any hint of remorse for killing his brother, he said to the Lord, "Today you are driving me from the land, and I will be hidden from your presence; I will be a restless wanderer on the earth, and whoever finds me will kill me" (Genesis 4:13-14).

Once again, God, who is rich in mercy (Ephesians 2:4), did not exact on Cain what he justly deserved. "But the Lord said to him [Cain], 'Not so; anyone who kills Cain will suffer vengeance seven times over.' Then the Lord put a mark on Cain so that no one who found him would kill him. So Cain went out from the Lord's presence and lived in the land of Nod, east of Eden" (Genesis 4:15-16).

Life continued for Cain. He married, had a son, built a city and named it after his son. A secular society apart from God emerged. We don't know anything about Cain's descendants until we come to a man named Lamech, who married two women. He is the first man to defy God's design of one man and one woman in marriage. He too killed a man and then boasted about it to his wives: "I have killed a man for wounding me, a young man for injuring me. If Cain is avenged seven times, then Lamech seventy-seven times" (Genesis 4:23-24). There is no sign of remorse, only a boastful proudness that seems to say, "If Cain got away with it, so can I."

But Cain did not get away with anything. His legacy has been handed down through the ages. If we listen carefully to some of those who have committed crimes or evil acts, they themselves cry "victim," and, like Cain, refuse to admit any culpability. God sees and knows everything, though, and one day "we must all appear before the judgment seat of Christ, so that each of us may receive what is due us for the things done while in the body, whether good or bad" (2 Corinthians 5:10).

Lord, forgive me for the times I have tried to get away with sin, thinking I could hide it from You. Your word tells us there is no place to hide from Your presence. Help me to be careful and do that which is pleasing in Your sight, that which honors You and puts me in right relationship with You, Lord of lords and King of kings. In Jesus' name, I pray. Amen.

Day 17

Hope is Not Lost

Genesis 4:25-26

After Abel's murder, Adam and Eve had another son named Seth, who had a son named Enosh. "At that time people began to call on the name of the Lord" (Genesis 4:26). What a blessed statement of hope that is.

We don't know how many children Adam and Eve ultimately had, but we know they had Cain, Abel, and Seth. Cain chose the way of the world. Abel and Seth chose the way of the Lord. These are the two choices we have in life.

Jesus said in Matthew 7:13-14, "Enter through the narrow gate. For wide is the gate and broad is the road that leads to destruction, and many enter through it. But small is the gate and narrow the road that leads to life, and only a few find it." Which will you choose?

When I began this study on the book of Genesis, I did not attribute such significance to Cain's actions. I've read this account many times, and I did not think about this being the actual broad road of which Jesus spoke that leads to destruction. It is, indeed, the path that's all about me, me, me and any benefits derived from "my" efforts are attributed to "me."

However, the way of Seth is the path of righteousness, which I believe leads to a relationship with Jesus. It is not always an easy path, but it is the path we must desire above all else to find true salvation (Acts 4:12).

Scripture tells us: "You will seek me and find me when you seek me with all of your heart" (Jeremiah 29:13). We are also told to "Seek the Lord while he may be found; call on him while he is near" (Isaiah 55:6). It is worth the effort because what we reap are the benefits of God's promises, which ultimately lead to an eternity in His presence.

Lord, when You spoke, Moses listened and he wrote Your story for us to read. Today, we are reaping the benefits of his choice to follow You with all his heart. Thank You for Your Word that guides me into Your truth. Help me to make wise choices that honor You and bring salvation, peace, and freedom to my life. In Jesus' name, I pray. Amen.

Day 18

Male and Female

Genesis 5:1-2

Today's Scripture may cause those who disagree with it, or find it offensive, to squirm like a worm on a fish hook. It also may be one of the reasons why some scientists and philosophers try to discredit not only this Scripture but the entire book of Genesis. If their efforts are successful, then the remainder of the Bible can also be tossed on the trash heap of history. Without the book of Genesis, the remainder of the Bible makes very little sense.

When I was growing up, referring to men when talking about a group of people often included women, and it wasn't offensive. My generation would never have believed that when we got into our sixties and seventies men could say they are women and women could say they are men, and those who disagree are labeled as hate-filled homophobes. I have not been confronted with having to address this subject personally and am not suggesting these feelings are not real. But I have also read articles from those who have tried "changing" genders and regretted it.[1]

I've considered not addressing this subject but in today's age of obsession with gender, same-sex legalized marriage, homosexuals adopting children, couples keeping the gender of their children secret and calling them "theybies,"[2] and a father being court-ordered not to call his son a boy[3], it is something that cannot be ignored. Our gender truly is at the very essence of who God made each and every one of us to be.

If we do not know who we are, then who are we?

It's interesting that a man can now say he's a woman, and vice versa, but why must a man or woman who thinks they are not a man or woman limit themselves to being the other gender? Why can't they be an animal or plant or anything else they want to be? I say this with all sincerity, not to poke fun or make a joke. To not know who we are brings nothing but confusion, and God is not the author of confusion (1 Corinthians 14:33).

If I am being politically incorrect, I make no apologies for believing what God said in Genesis 5:2. It comes down to what the Bible is all about: Will we be who God has chosen us to be or will we choose our own way?

Lord, before he was born, You told Jeremiah (1:5), "Before I formed you in the womb I knew you, before you were born I set you apart; I appointed you as a prophet to the nations." Jeremiah was not the only one You spoke to about this (Psalm 139:13-16 and Judges 13:3-5). May each and every one who seeks You come to know and understand that what You said to Jeremiah and others is true for me; that You knew me before I was born; You knew whether I would be male or female, and You have a plan and purpose for my life. In Jesus' name, I pray. Amen.

Day 19

From Adam to Noah

Genesis 5:3-32

From Adam came Seth, Enosh, Kenan, Mahalel, Jared and Enoch, the father of Methuselah. "Enoch walked faithfully with God 300 years and had other sons and daughters. Altogether, Enoch lived a total of 365 years. Enoch walked faithfully with God; then he was no more, because God took him away" (Genesis 5:22-24).

Amidst the evil and sin which existed in the world, the knowledge of God was handed down in such a way that one man, Enoch, was righteous enough to pass over from life on earth to heaven without physically dying. We are not told much else about Enoch except that he pleased God (Hebrews 11:5), and that he prophesied about evil men (Jude 14-16). Is it possible his words were so despised that God took him before he too was murdered? Perhaps, but only God knows for certain.

After some extensive research, I thought I'd found a meaning for Methuselah's name, but after delving a little further I've come to the conclusion that there is no consensus. *Answers in Genesis* is a great source for detailed information on the book of Genesis. So, I decided to include one citation, if you would like some insight into the meaning of Methuselah's name.[1]

What we do know about Methuselah is that he is recorded as the longest living human being in history at 969 years old. Hence, the saying, "He's as old as Methuselah."[2] Methuselah was the father of Lamech (a different Lamech than the line of Cain), and Lamech was the father of Noah, who was the father of Shem, Ham, and Japheth. When Methuselah died, the flood came, and, oh, what a flood it was!

Lord, thank You for our rich heritage from the beginning of creation. We have been adopted into Your family as Your sons and daughters through Jesus Christ, Your Son. Because of Your Word, we know the lineage of Jesus to which we belong. Help me live in the heritage You have given me and help me teach my children so they may teach their children. Who knows that, one day, they may walk with You and be no more because they have crossed over from this life into eternity. In Jesus' name, I pray. Amen.

Day 20

One Person Makes a Difference

Genesis 6:1-8:17

If you're ever in Williamstown, Kentucky, be sure and visit the Ark Encounter, a life-size reconstruction of Noah's Ark.[1] This massive structure housed Noah, his family, and at least two of every kind of animal. It gives us an inkling of what life must have been like during the flood that wiped out every living thing on the face of the earth. There is enough information contained in this one place to assuage the doubts of even the most ardent unbelievers.

"Now the earth was corrupt in God's sight and was full of violence...So God said to Noah, '...So make yourself an ark of cypress wood...'" (Genesis 6:11, and 13-14).

If God said to you, "I want you to build an ark," what would have been your response in the midst of such corruption and violence? Be totally honest. No judgment here.

I'd like to think my answer would have been an enthusiastic, get-out-my-hammer-and-nails "yes!" But even as I write today's devotion, I feel a tug of hesitancy in my spirit, apprehension, maybe even a touch of fear. But not Noah. He got right to work, and "did everything just as God commanded him" (Genesis 6:22).

"Noah was a righteous man, blameless among the people of his time, and he walked faithfully with God" (Genesis 6:9). Wouldn't you like that to be said about you? I sure would!

Amidst all the wickedness of the human race, where every inclination of the thoughts of the human heart was only evil, one man stood out. Even though the heart of God Almighty was deeply troubled and He regretted ever making human beings, He found one person so dedicated to Him that his wife, their three sons and their wives, also believed in God. There is so much to this story, the details of which could take an entire book to explore, but my focus will be on Noah, the one righteous man God found in all the Earth to save the human race.

Have you ever thought about how difficult life was for Noah and his family as they no doubt endured endless snide remarks, laughter and jeering? It seems impossible, doesn't it? Yet, because of God's love and mercy, they were able to persevere, hoping against hope that others would join them before it was too late. But none did, and the flood came and covered the entire earth with water, and "every living thing that moved on land perished" (Genesis 7:21).

The parallels of the flood and salvation through Christ are many; one of which is that one person makes a difference. Because Noah was faithful, God saved the human race. Unfortunately, sin was not eradicated with the flood. Even though it was a new beginning, it wasn't long until the Earth was repopulated and evil once again reared its ugly head. As we will learn, though, God made a promise to Noah, and He has kept that promise to this very day. Thankfully, one person who was fully God and fully man, Jesus Christ, fulfilled God's plan to redeem humanity from sin and evil. "God made him who had no sin to be sin for us, so that in him we might become the righteousness of God" (2 Corinthians 5:21).

We have a story to tell. Just like in the days of Noah, most will not listen, but we can find comfort in knowing "there is rejoicing in the presence of the angels of God over *one* sinner who repents" (Luke 15:10). I italicize "one" because if just one person hears the message of salvation that Jesus brought and believes it, it is worth rejoicing over!

Lord, help me be that one person who, like Noah, does everything just as You command. Help me recognize Your voice and be the one who responds without hesitancy so that, like Noah, others will respond to You as well. May my life be the one that brings honor, glory, and praise to You now and forevermore. In Jesus' name, I pray. Amen.

Day 21

Putting God First

Genesis 8:18-22

Don't you know the feel of sunshine on their faces and the smell of fresh air was welcomed after months of being cooped up in the ark with smelly, noisy animals. Noah and his family were about to step on to dry land, which would be a funny feeling after riding the waves of the flood for so long. Life would not be like it was before God closed the door to the ark and the waters began to cover the Earth.

Noah wasted no time honoring God for bringing them through the storm. The first thing he did was build "an altar to the Lord and, taking some of all the clean animals and clean birds, he sacrificed burnt offerings on it. The Lord smelled the pleasing aroma and said in his heart, 'Never again will I curse the ground because of humans, even though every inclination of the human heart is evil from childhood. And never again will I destroy all living creatures, as I have done'" (Genesis 8:20-21).

Just as the smell of sacrificial animals and birds was a pleasing aroma to God, "Christ loved us and gave himself up for us as a fragrant offering and sacrifice to God" (Ephesians 5:2).

The people of the Earth had become so wicked that God destroyed them with a flood. Now He vowed to never destroy humans by flood again, even though "every inclination of the human heart is evil from childhood."

Was the blood sacrifice of animals by Noah an atonement for the sins of mankind, perhaps bringing about this promise from God? I'm not certain of the answer, but I do know blood was shed when animals were killed because of sin in the garden of Eden (Genesis 3:21), and Abel offered fat portions from some of the firstborn of his flock to the Lord (Genesis 4:4), which would have required shedding the animal's blood. But when Christ came into the world, He made the ultimate sacrifice for us when He said, "Sacrifice and offering you did not desire, but a body you prepared for me; with burnt offerings and sin offerings you were not pleased." Then He said, "Here I am—it is written about me in the scroll—I have come to do your will, my God" (Hebrews 10:5-7). "And by that will, we have been made holy through the sacrifice of the body of Jesus Christ once for all" (Hebrews 10:10).

By putting God first in his life, Noah's obedience made it possible for the human race to continue; and Christ's obedience on the cross made it possible for us to be put back into relationship with our Creator (Romans 5:11).

Lord, help me put You first in my life, as Noah did, setting aside all the things that constantly vie for my attention. Help me also to remember the sacrifice Jesus made for me by shedding His blood for my sins. In Jesus' name, I pray. Amen.

Day 22

A New Covenant with a Sign

Genesis 9:1-17

God blessed Noah and his sons, saying to them, "Be fruitful and increase in number; fill the earth," similar to the words He earlier spoke to Adam (Genesis 1:28). It was a new beginning for Noah and his family. Before the flood, animals were not fearful of people but now they would be; and everything that lived and moved would now be food to eat, except for "meat that has its lifeblood still in it" (Genesis 9:4).

The Lord gave Noah instructions on how to set up a system of government, which included giving an accounting when one man killed another. Unlike Cain and Lamech, who were not put to death for their murders, God told Noah, "Whoever sheds human blood, by humans shall their blood be shed; for in the image of God has God made mankind" (Genesis 9:6). Now if someone were found guilty of murder, their own life would be forfeited, and the punishment would be meted out by a person, not by God.

These things were established, for God made a promise that "As long as the earth endures, seedtime and harvest, cold and heat, summer and winter, day and night will never cease" (Genesis 8:22). He would never flood the whole earth again!

Then, as a reminder to Himself and as a sign of His covenant with all generations to come, God said to Noah, "I have set my rainbow in the clouds...This is the sign of the covenant I have established between me and all life on the earth" (Genesis 9:13 and 17).

I once survived a horrific storm with thunder and lightning, high winds and sheets of rain which left debris scattered everywhere. When it was finally over, I looked out my bedroom window and saw a double rainbow so brilliant it lit up the entire sky. It was so unusual, there was a report of it on the nightly news. As I gazed out at this beautiful sight, I thought back to God's promise and was thankful that though we too experience the storms of life, the rainbow that follows reminds us God's promises are true and the covenant He made so long ago still remains. And it will remain until there is a new heaven and a new earth, "for the first heaven and the first earth had passed away, and there was no longer any sea" (Revelation 21:1).

This will be the new beginning we are longing for, and it will be everlasting! The apostle John wrote about it when he said this: "And I heard a loud voice from the throne saying, 'Look! God's dwelling place is now among the people, and he will dwell with them. They will be his people, and God himself will be with them and be their God. He will wipe every tear from their eyes. There will be no more death or mourning or crying or pain, for the old order of things has passed away'" (Revelation 21:3-4).

Lord, I ask that You keep me in covenant with You all the days of my life, remembering that after every storm there is a rainbow. In Jesus' name, I pray. Amen.

Day 23

No Restraint

Genesis 9:18-21

The Lord declares in Scripture, "For my thoughts are not your thoughts; neither are your ways my ways" (Isaiah 55:8). When I consider what this means, I realize God alone is good and no fault can be found in Him. He is righteous, just, merciful, faithful, trustworthy. When He created the world and everything in it, He saw that it was good. It wasn't until the human beings He created disobeyed Him, by basically saying, *We know better than you do, God*, that evil entered God's perfect creation. Even Noah, who the Bible tells us was a righteous man, who came off the ark and built an altar to God, sinned, which resulted in severe consequences for generations to come.

I love that what is written in the Bible does not sugarcoat the lives of God's people in the Old Testament by leaving out their disobedience and sin, because it lets us know that they too were not perfect. It also shows God wants us to know, in His loving way, that this is why we need a Savior.

Not long after leaving the ark, Noah tilled the soil, planted a vineyard and made wine, which he then drank. There's nothing in the Bible that prohibits the drinking of wine. It is getting drunk that's the problem, and that is exactly what Noah did.

Have you ever been drunk? I have. It's not something I'm proud of. Though I was not of legal drinking age, I worked in the liquor store that my dad owned, and we often had alcohol in our home. It was very accessible and there were times I took advantage of that. Also, during my high school years there were lots of parties which included not only alcohol but drugs. I wish now I hadn't done it, but I did. Getting drunk often leads to behavior we would never participate in if we were sober.

It was no different with Noah. He not only got drunk, but he laid "uncovered inside his tent" (Genesis 9:21). The implications of this in the Hebrew language means some type of sexual perversion.[1][2] So it wasn't just a matter of getting drunk and being naked.

We have restraints in life that are instilled in us at a young age, from sources such as our upbringing, our conscience, laws enacted by the state, any number of things. Take away those restraints with things like drugs and alcohol, and we discover what we are really like. It's usually not a very pretty picture, either.

True restraint comes by the grace of God. "For the grace of God has appeared that offers salvation to all people. It teaches us to say 'No' to ungodliness and worldly passions, and to live self-controlled, upright and godly lives in this present age" (Titus 2:11-12)

Perhaps Noah got carried away and thought his accomplishments were of his own making. For whatever reason, he sinned, which brought a curse on Ham's son Canaan, as we will soon discover.

What we can learn from this is that we are all sinners, even righteous Noah. "If we claim to be without sin, we deceive ourselves and the truth is not in us. If we confess our sins, he is faithful and just and will forgive us our sins and purify us from all unrighteousness" (1 John 1:8-9).

Lord, I pray never to forget that it is by Your grace I have been saved from the ravages of sin. Help me not to be tempted by the ways of this world which continually entice me to turn from You. I ask for Your strength to fight the good fight in order to remain holy and righteous in Your sight. In Jesus' name, I pray, Amen.

Day 24

Gazing and Gossiping

Genesis 9:22-23

What came next in the unfolding events of life after the flood is that Noah got drunk and Ham went into his father's tent and looked upon his nakedness—we are told, actually, that he gazed; meaning he lingered, looking long at him. Then, as though to disgrace his father further, he left the tent and gossiped unashamedly to his brothers about what he had seen.

Shem was appalled by this and enlisted the help of his brother Japheth to take a garment and lay it across their shoulders. Then they walked into the tent backward and covered their father's nakedness without turning to look at him.

The Bible says to flee temptation (2 Timothy 2:22-26), which means to do an about-face as though you had run into a brick wall. Turn around and run as fast as your feet will carry you, run into the arms of Jesus, the one who gives us the strength and ability to do all things through Him (Philippians 4:13).

If we can grasp this concept—that we are unable to do life in our own strength and ability—and take hold of Jesus like we would a life preserver, never letting go, we will be able to stand firm until the end and be saved (Matthew 24:13). We are overcomers through the One in whom "we live and move and have our being" (Acts 17:28).

Ham's choice was to go his own way, and the result of his actions trickles down throughout the entirety of the Old Testament, which we will read about time and again. But let's not forget Shem, who chose God's way and through whom came the Savior of the world (Luke 3:38).

Lord, I cannot thank You enough for giving us Your story, for revealing to us the mystery of life as it unfolds before our very eyes. You have not only given us the history of creation, but you tell us what to expect for the future. What a blessed generation we are, to have it all written down in one book to read over and over again. Help me to hide Your Word in my heart so that I will not sin against You. In Jesus' name, I pray. Amen.

Day 25

Cursed Again

Genesis 9:24-25

Noah was angry when he awoke from his wine and discovered what Ham had done, so much so he said, "Cursed be Canaan! The lowest of slaves will he be to his brothers" (Genesis 9:25).

There are diverse opinions among biblical scholars as to why Noah cursed Ham's son, Canaan, and not Ham; too many for me to expound on any of them, actually. My thought is this was more than just an angry old man who was upset that his son had seen him naked, gazing at him and then gossiping to his brothers about it. I believe what Noah saw in his son was the wretchedness that would take place in the years to come and spread all throughout history. Perhaps he even saw his own weakness, which would be passed down to future generations.

Whatever the reason, Noah had been found righteous in God's sight and He was willing to start all over with him and his family, knowing that sin was still a part of their human nature.

Our take-away from this should be that getting drunk is never good. It is better to be in complete control of our thoughts and actions, and the way for us to do this is to fix our thoughts and eyes on Jesus. He is the only sinless man who ever walked the face of the earth, and "God made him who had no sin to be sin for us, so that in him we might become the righteousness of God" (2 Corinthians 5:21).

These are not just words written on a page to read for our enjoyment. They are the truth of God which continually reveals the two choices in life: God's way or our own way. The way of Ham, as the way of Cain, leads to the wide path of destruction which Jesus spoke of; the way of Shem, the way of Seth, is the narrow path which ultimately leads to life everlasting.

Lord, at this point I am without words to even write as I am overwhelmed with the cohesiveness of Your revelation through Your Word. Teach me Your ways, instill in me Your righteousness, that I may choose the way of Shem, the way of Jesus, the way of everlasting life with You. In Jesus' name, I pray. Amen.

Day 26

The Blessing

Genesis 9:26-28

As a father, there's no doubt Noah had great expectations for his sons' futures. It certainly could not have brought him pleasure to speak a curse on the succeeding generation of his son, Ham. When it came to Shem and Japheth, Noah must have felt some joy in blessing them. They had showed respect to their father by refusing to look at his nakedness and instead covered him.

We know, through Noah's blessings, Shem was in relationship with God and would continue to be through the generations. The genealogies written in Luke 3 reveal that Shem's descendants are the Jews, from whom came Jesus, the Savior of the world (John 3:16-18).

Through my research, I've discovered I did not fully understand the significance of the curse and the blessing. Now I realize they were not a one-time thing but something that affected succeeding generations. This is why reading the Bible is important to our Christian faith. Even if we've read particular passages numerous times, it's not unusual to learn something new each time.

We are told the Word of God is alive and active (Hebrews 4:12), which means it's not some ancient manuscript with no value to our present day. It has as much meaning, purpose, and significance to those who are living today as it did when it was written. Jesus is alive! He sits at the Father's right hand and intercedes for us (Hebrews 7:25). This news should bring excitement and joy to our souls. We can know Him intimately, and we can pray to Him. He hears us, listens to us, and knows our every need before we even ask (Matthew 6:8).

I am thankful for Noah's blessing upon Shem, a blessing that is still alive and well for those who believe in Jesus as Lord and Savior.

Lord, when I consider Your heavens and the work of Your hands, I am in awe that You love me; that You care about my life and have a plan and purpose for it. I pray I will come to know the incomparable power of Your riches and the blessings You have promised from before the creation of the world so that I may come to know You and serve You in a real and personal way. In Jesus' name, I pray. Amen.

Day 27

Be Fruitful and Fill the Earth

Genesis 9:29-10:32

Noah lived to be 950 years. That is difficult to comprehend. If someone lives to be 100 or older today, it's newsworthy. We don't know if Noah and his wife had more children after the flood. If they did, they are not accounted for in the genealogy. We do know Noah's three sons had children. Coming out of the ark and realizing they were the only eight people on the entire earth and were responsible for repopulation must have been daunting!

Japheth had seven sons; Ham had four sons; and Shem had five sons. From these people came many more sons and daughters, some of whom became nations. From Japheth came the maritime peoples who spread out into their territories by their clans with their nations. From Ham came Nimrod, who grew to be a mighty warrior on the earth and established a kingdom from which some of the first cities came. He built Nineveh, a place referred to later in the Old Testament. Also from Ham came the Canaanite people, who are mentioned many times throughout the Old Testament as being at odds with God's chosen people, the descendants of Shem.

One of Shem's sons was named Eber, from the Hebrew verb "abar," meaning "to cross over" or "to pass through."[1] From Eber comes the word "Hebrew,"[2] who are the Jews, the chosen people of God. These are the clans of Noah's sons. From these clans descended all peoples who began to spread out and fill the earth after the flood.

Lord, You and You alone know my beginning and my ending. I am not my own, though I often think I am. Some people are proud of their heritage and ancestry; still, others have no knowledge of theirs. No matter a person's family history, Lord, help me remember You are the Creator. In Jesus' name, I pray. Amen.

Day 28

The Spoken Word

Genesis 11:1-9

Language: it's the words we speak and how we communicate with one another. Of all God's creation, humans are the only ones who do this. According to Ethnologue[1], there are about 7,111 languages spoken around the entire world, and that doesn't include the different dialects. I love languages and wish I could speak them all, but that would be impossible. Have you ever wondered where all these languages come from? Let's look at today's Scripture to find the answer.

There was a time when the whole earth had a common language and one speech. As all the people came together, they decided to build a tower to heaven so they could make a name for themselves and not be scattered over the face of the earth. It wasn't long before God quickly put an end to the very thing they wanted to accomplish. Their desire was to make a name for themselves, something which many people do today by seeking fame and fortune.

There was so much power when all the people spoke one language. The Lord said they could accomplish anything. Because of this, He also said, "Come, let us go down and confuse their language so they will not understand each other" (Genesis 11:7). Thus, the division among the people of the earth.

They stopped building this tower to themselves when the Lord confused their language so they could not understand each other. Then He scattered them over all the earth.

In the movie *The Bible,* there is a scene depicting the Tower of Babel. It is mass confusion as people speak but cannot understand each other. Eventually, small groups joined together and then wandered in different directions, never again to be one people with a common language.

God's desire was not for all the peoples of the earth to remain in one place and make a name for themselves. He had greater plans for humanity. They were to fulfill His will for His creation by multiplying and filling the Earth. This divine act of scattering separated humanity into distinctive ethnic and language groups.[2]

We are told in 1 Corinthians, "But whoever is united with the Lord is one with him in spirit" (6:17). It is in this spirit of unity, which brings honor to God, that we once again speak the same language and become, as Jesus prayed, one with the Father, Son, and Holy Spirit (John 17:21-22).

Heavenly Father, give me wisdom this day to think before I speak and to use my language effectively to lift up others. In Jesus' name, I pray. Amen.

Day 29
A Rich Heritage

Genesis 11:10-26

My mom had a passion for genealogy. In her research, she not only discovered previously unknown facts about our family, she traced her side back to William Brewster who came to America on the Mayflower. She spent hours going through records and getting documentation to prove this. Because of her efforts, I was able to apply for membership in the General Society of Mayflower Descendants. It was humbling to learn that one of our ancestors actually survived that arduous journey across the open seas.

My mom also told me we had ancestors from Kentucky. When she and my aunt visited us in Tennessee, we took a couple of days to drive there and check it out. We found what she was looking for at the county clerk's office. It's an amazing experience to go to a courthouse or someplace where records are kept and find the names of your ancestors, as well as information about who they married, where they lived, and what property they owned. It's like discovering a new part of yourself. This is also how I felt when I began reading Matthew, the first book of the New Testament.

The first chapter begins with the genealogy of Jesus Christ, going all the way back to Abraham, who we will read and learn about. As I studied His genealogy, even memorized it, I went back to the Old Testament and found the names of those referred to in Jesus's genealogy. Yes, they existed! It all began with Abraham, who was appointed by God to be the father of a chosen people (the Jews). By Abraham, all the nations of the world would be blessed. Because of Abraham's faithfulness, we have a rich heritage when we become followers of Jesus Christ (Romans 8:16-17 and John 1:12-13).

Thank You, heavenly Father, for sending Jesus. Because of His death and resurrection, I have new life by Your Spirit and am now Your child. What a rich heritage You have given me. Watch over me as a parent watches their child. Help me to love and obey You. In Jesus' name, I pray. Amen.

DAY 30

THE CALL TO CANAAN

Genesis 11:27-32

Searching through God's word is like looking for precious gems and metals, even oil, none of which are found on the earth's surface. To reap their benefits, an arduous process of mining and digging has to take place, first to find these products, harvest them, and ultimately prepare them for their intended use.

When we dig deep into the Bible, there are many precious gems waiting to be discovered, but it takes time, along with a strong desire to find them (1 Chronicles 28:9). One of those gems is Abram (later named Abraham). He was the son of Terah, whose genealogy goes back to Shem, the son of Noah. This genealogy is important because it takes us all the way back to Adam (Luke 3:23-38).

"The Lord had said to Abram, 'Go from your country, your people and your father's household to the land I will show you. I will make you into a great nation, and I will bless you... I will bless those who bless you, and whoever curses you I will curse; and all peoples on earth will be blessed through you'" (Genesis 12:1-3.) Abram obeyed God and went (Hebrews 11:8).

On the way from Ur (where God called Abram), Terah, his father, wanted to stop in Harran, halfway between Ur and Canaan (where God called Abram to go), and they settled there. We're not told why. Perhaps Terah became sentimental because the name of this town was similar to his son Haran (Lot's father), who died. Or perhaps it was because it was the end of the known Chaldean civilization with all of its modern amenities and going any further meant going into the unknown. No matter the reason, this wasn't where God intended Abram to stop and put down roots.

Isn't this what sometimes happens to us? We ask Jesus to become our Savior, leaving our past life behind, yet for whatever reason we don't nurture our relationship with Him. We don't take the time necessary to dig deep into God's word, and so we miss the incomparable great riches He has in store for us, even here on earth (Ephesians 2:6-7).

All during their time in Harran, we have no mention of God speaking to Abram. It wasn't until he was seventy-five years old, after his father died, that Abram continued the journey to Canaan. It was then God appeared to him and said, "To your offspring I will give this land" (Genesis 12:7).

Do you ever wonder why you don't hear from the Lord? Could it be you are stuck in Harran after He told you to go to Canaan? If so, why would He give further guidance if you haven't even traveled the distance He told you to go?

It wasn't until Abram took the next step and reached his destination that God once again began to speak to him.

Lord, help me go the distance You've ask me to travel. Help me not to stop before I arrive, for I want to hear Your voice and receive Your direction so that my life will honor You. In Jesus' name, I pray. Amen.

Day 31

Making it Right

Genesis 12:1-10

TV news is notorious for reporting bad and often sad news stories, so much so I rarely watch it except to check the local weather. Our conversations often gravitate to negative things, such as that which is wrong in our world, causing us to worry. It's rare to hear good news stories or find solutions for things that are wrong in order to make them right.

As Christians, we know what is wrong with our world. We also know how to make it right. We know "Salvation is found in no one else [other than Jesus], for there is no other name under heaven given to mankind by which we must be saved" (Acts 4:12).

Yet, when a Christian offers this solution, they are sometimes met with resistance, even anger; and may be called names such as racist, homophobic, or bigot. Those hearing the salvation message might feel like they are hearing someone yell fire in a crowded theater. All they want to do is run away as fast and far as they can, not realizing a real and personal relationship with Jesus is what makes life right. They prefer to live life on their own terms, often to their detriment, rather than hear the one true solution that will set them free from the sin that so easily entangles us (Hebrews 12:1). How odd that the answer to life is rejected as foolishness by many people (1 Corinthians 1:18).

Perhaps that's how it was in the days leading up to Abram. Before God chose him, there were a few people mentioned in the first eleven chapters of the Bible as believing in God. When we get to Chapter 12 and beyond, the focus changes from many peoples and languages to just one man named Abram, whose faith in God was credited to him as righteousness (Romans 4:1-5). As we will discover, he not only became the father of all nations who were and are blessed because of him, he is also known as a friend of God (James 2:23).

From Adam, who brought sin into the world, to the flood, up to the confounding of languages and all the things that were wrong with the world, the focus now turns to one man through whom God's plan of redemption flows. From this point forward the salvation message unfolds, showing people how to put their life right with God.

Lord, open my heart to Your message. Give me Your understanding and wisdom so that I too may do my part in making things right. In Jesus' name, I pray. Amen.

Day 32

To Egypt and Back

Genesis 12:10-20

When Abram and his family arrived in Canaan, God told him, "To your offspring, I will give this land" (Genesis 12:7). At the time, his wife Sarai was barren, and he might have wondered how that would happen. He built an altar to the Lord when he arrived, but apparently he wasn't quite ready to wholeheartedly receive the plan God had in store. He saw the land was inhabited and there was a famine, so he headed to Egypt rather than the land of Canaan. When he got there, he was afraid for his life and conspired with Sarai to tell Pharaoh they were brother and sister, which was half true but still a lie.

While in Egypt, Abram acquired a large amount of livestock, as well as camels, menservants, and maidservants. But trouble was brewing in Pharaoh's palace because of Sarai, whom Pharaoh had taken into his harem. When Pharaoh discovered the truth, he was furious and confronted Abram, "What have you done to me? Why didn't you tell me she [Sarai] was your wife?...Now then, here is your wife. Take her and go" (Genesis 12:18-19).

Abram left Pharaoh, and then wandered from place to place until he came to the area between Bethel and Ai, where he had been earlier and where he first built an altar to the Lord. It was there Abram again called on the name of the Lord.

We have no account of God speaking to Abram while in Egypt, but He did speak to Pharaoh. When Pharaoh discovered the truth, he counted himself more righteous than Abram, who left Egypt in disgrace but returned to the place where he came from and called on the name of the Lord. We know God answered Abram because this is not the end; it's actually just the beginning, for Abram was getting closer to where God wanted him to be.

The Lord isn't looking for perfection in His people. None exists, except in Christ (Hebrews 7:28). We read this time and again throughout the Old and New Testaments. We all have faults, but when we come to the place of repentance, He forgives our sins and cleanses us from those faults, bringing us into restored communion with Him (1 John 1:9). This is what Abram did, and God restored him.

Lord, help me come back to You when I wander off. Forgive me, heal me, and restore me to You. In Jesus' name, I pray. Amen.

Day 33

Ur, Harran and Canaan

Reading about places like Ur, Harran, Canaan and Egypt, you might be asking, "What significance do these places have to me today?" Though these may have been physical towns and countries on a map, they are much more than that when we consider what they represented. Ur was Abram's hometown. Everything and everyone he knew was there. He would have been familiar with his surroundings and been comfortable; yet God called him to leave this place.

How about you? Are you in a comfortable place right now? Is everything going well? You might even be thinking you don't need God's help because you are able to take care of things yourself. But is there a tug at your heart that God is calling you to something deeper, something beyond yourself? Is He asking you to get up and follow Him? Are you willing, or would you rather enjoy your comforts and stay where you are?

Harran is the place where Abram settled for a time because his father did not want to continue traveling. This is not where God told Abram to settle, but he listened to his dad and stayed there. What about you? Do you allow the wants and desires of others to overrule what God has called you to? Are you content to be in a place where others want you, missing out on hearing from God because you are not where He wants you to be?

Then there's Canaan, the Promised Land, the place where the Lord appeared to Abram and said, "To your offspring, I will give this land" (Genesis 12:7). Abram built an altar there to the Lord. Later, in Bethel, he built another altar to the Lord and called upon His name. As Abram got closer, he realized it wasn't going to be handed to him on a silver platter. He saw the land was occupied by others and there was even a severe famine. As we read yesterday, he went to Egypt, a place of wealth and prosperity, apparently unaffected by the famine.

There is no indication he prayed about this decision, and as we read the events more closely, we discover something else. As Abram got closer to Egypt, he feared for his life. He asked his wife Sarai to tell Pharaoh she was his sister instead of his wife. He went so far as to put her in jeopardy to save his own skin, which she agreed to.

Abram prospered greatly while in Egypt. But when Pharaoh discovered the truth, he banished Abram from Egypt in disgrace. This might be a good time to ask yourself, "Am I being totally honest and upright about everything in my life? Or have I allowed my own desires and ambitions to take precedence over what God is saying to me, putting not only myself in jeopardy but others?"

The wonderful thing is that Abram realized the errors of his ways and returned to Canaan, the place where God called him, the place where he first built an altar. There, Abram called on the name of the Lord. This is where all of us should strive to be, the place where God wants us, the place where He guides us by the gentleness of His Spirit, and we have no fear because He is with us (Psalm 34:4).

Lord, bring me to the place where You want me to be and keep me from wandering, especially when times get rough. In Jesus' name, I pray. Amen.

Day 34

Abram and Lot Separate

Genesis 13

The things we acquire in our own abilities don't always benefit us when it comes to trusting the Lord. Life goes much better when we allow Him to provide for us, which is why Abram and Lot should have left behind all they gained in Egypt. Instead, they brought all their wealth and slaves with them. By the time they arrived back in Canaan, this caused quarreling and dissension between their herdsmen because there wasn't enough land to support them if they all stayed together.

This quarreling left them vulnerable to the Canaanites and Perezites, who were also living in the land at the time. If Abram and Lot couldn't agree among themselves, how would they be strong enough to ward off any attacks from their enemies?

"So Abram said to Lot, 'Let's not have any quarreling between you and me...for we are close relatives...Let's part company. If you go to the left, I'll go to the right; if you go to the right, I'll go to the left.' Lot looked around and saw that the whole plain of Jordan toward Zoar was well watered, like the garden of the Lord" (Genesis 13:8-10), and that's what he chose. He wanted what looked like the best of the land.

For the first time since leaving Ur, Abram was where the Lord wanted him, all to Himself. "The Lord said to Abram after Lot had parted from him, 'Look around from where you are, to the north and south, to the east and west. All the land that you see I will give to you and your offspring forever...Go, walk through the length and breadth of the land, for I am giving it to you.' So Abram went to live near the great trees of Mamre at Hebron, where he pitched his tents. There he built an altar to the Lord" (Genesis 13:14-18).

Family is one of the strongest bonds we have. It is not easy to let go of those we love but, when it interferes with God's plan, we sometimes have to make a choice. It wasn't easy for Abram but he did it, and we can, too.

Lord, I have often leaned on my own strength and understanding to gain what I thought was necessary for my own wellbeing. Forgive me for not looking to You as the source of my provision. Help me do better each day and trust You for all my needs. You know what they are even before I ask. In Jesus' name, I pray. Amen.

Day 35

Abram Rescues Lot

Genesis 14:1-16

Time passed after Abram and Lot went their separate ways. Life was going well for Abram, but down in the fertile valley trouble was brewing. Rebellion was in the air in Sodom and the surrounding cities which were controlled by chiefs and kings. When those kings got wind of the rebellion, they banded together and pounced on the people like a lion overtaking its prey. In the first recorded war in the Bible, the kings not only took the goods from these cities, but all the people were hauled away, including Lot and his family (Genesis 14:1-12).

When Abram got the news, he didn't sit back and say, "Well, look at old Lot; he got what he deserved. Why should I do anything to help him?" His first thoughts were not of himself but of his nephew and family, who were taken prisoner and carted away from their homes.

With lightning speed, before the enemy even knew what hit them, Abram called the 318 trained men born in his household, and together they went to rescue Lot and his family. God gave Abram the victory, after which the king of Sodom came to meet Abram in the Valley of Shaveh and offered all the recaptured goods to Abram. This encounter seems to indicate Abram came to realize his blessings were from God and God alone, and he did not need or even desire anyone else's riches. He learned a lot from his years in Harran and Egypt. Now that he was in the place where God wanted him, he was not going to risk losing it.

Where do you find yourself in your walk with God? Do you depend on yourself, or others, for your provision? Do you spend countless hours worrying about what you don't have? Do you work so many hours you neglect your home and family, and then complain because you never hear from God? Maybe it's time to take a deep breath, count your blessings, and begin relying on the Lord God Most High, Creator of heaven and earth. He will bring you to the place He wants you to be so that, like Abram, He can provide all that you need.

Lord, You alone know my needs, my wants, and my desires. May I come to the place where I rely on You to fill them all, giving You and You alone the praise You are worthy to receive. In Jesus' name, I pray. Amen.

Day 36

Melchizedek, The Mysterious

Genesis 14:17-24

Undertaking this study on Genesis has at times overwhelmed me with a flood of emotions, especially when a passage has significance, yet it's difficult to fully comprehend what that significance is. Such is the case with Melchizedek, King of Salem. After Abram's victory, we are introduced to Melchizedek, "the mysterious." I say "mysterious" because he appears on the scene suddenly, and other than Psalm 110 he is not mentioned again in the Old Testament. Yet in the New Testament, we are told he is "without father or mother, without genealogy, without beginning of days or end of life, resembling the Son of God, he remains a priest forever" (Hebrews 7:3).

In his brief encounter with Abram, Melchizedek served him bread and wine. This could have been for the purpose of renewal and refreshment, for surely Abram was exhausted from the battle on his return journey home. It could also represent what took place later in the New Testament when Jesus served communion to his disciples at the last Passover meal before his crucifixion (Matthew 26:26-28).

Melchizedek gave a blessing to Abram, which he said was from God Most High who delivered Abram's enemies into his hands. After this, Abram gave a tenth of everything he won in the battle to Melchizedek, something now referred to as "the tithe."

My understanding from listening to hours of sermons, doing research and spending time in prayer, is that Melchizedek was the prophetic symbol in the Old Testament of who Christ is in the New Testament. His appearance to Abram signified the eternal and everlasting "royal priesthood" that now comes through

Jesus Christ, who died for our sins once for all, who was raised from the dead, and who is now seated at the right hand of God and intercedes for us (Romans 8:34).

While Abram was the father of God's promise in the Old Testament and was blessed by Melchizedek, it is Jesus who is perfect forever and is the fulfillment of that promise in the New Testament. Jesus is a priest forever in the order of Melchizedek (Hebrews 7:11 and Psalm 110:4).

Lord, open my heart and mind to the meaning of Your word this day. Give me the wisdom and revelation I need so that I might know You better, You who are God Almighty and the One who lives forever and ever! In Jesus' name, I pray. Amen.

Day 37

Righteousness

Genesis 15:1-6

During a somewhat heated conversation with a family member who isn't convinced the Bible is the Word of God, he told me emphatically, "I am righteous." The neurons in my brain began to race in all directions when I heard that statement, and I was unable to give a response. I thought of one later, but it was too late. That seems to happen to me more than I care to admit. We ended our conversation agreeing to disagree, and I hung up the phone shaking my head and wondering out loud, "What does he base his righteousness on?" Unfortunately, we never revisited that conversation, at least not yet, but understanding righteousness and how we attain it brings us back to the life of Abram.

We know that although Abram listened to God, he wasn't perfect. He lied to Pharaoh to save his own skin and, instead of going directly to the Promised Land, he dawdled along the way. It's probable to assume he learned lessons from these mistakes as he talked with God about what troubled him, such as having no heir to pass down the promise that his offspring would be like the dust of the earth (Genesis 13:16). God reiterated His promise when He took Abram outside his tent and said, "Look up at the sky and count the stars—if indeed you can count them...So shall your offspring be" (Genesis 15:5).

The words that follow are the beginning of the hope that intricately winds its way through the entirety of the Bible: "Abram believed the Lord, and he credited it to him as righteousness" (Genesis 15:6). In other words, because Abram, in his heart of hearts, believed what God told him, even though circumstances pointed in another direction, God blotted out all the wrongdoing that took place in Abram's life and credited his belief in Him as righteousness: "that which is morally right; just; upright; equitable; especially, free from wrong, guilt or sin; virtuous; worthy."[1] That is pretty powerful.

There is no other religion on earth that gives that kind of freedom from sin. There is more, though: "The words 'it was credited to him' were written not for him alone, but also for us, to whom God will credit righteousness—for us who believe in him who raised Jesus our Lord from the dead" (Romans 4:23-24).

Our righteousness comes through belief in the One who not only died for our sins but was raised to life. We don't make ourselves righteous, but it is credited to us as righteousness when we believe in Jesus Christ as our Lord and Savior. What a hope, what a promise, and it all began with Abram who at eighty-six years of age believed what God said.

Lord, search me and know my ways. If there is anything hidden deep within me that prevents me from fully believing in You with all my heart, take it from me. Like Abram, may I believe what You say, without question, so that it will be credited to me as righteousness. In Jesus' name, I pray. Amen.

Day 38

God's Faithfulness

Genesis 15:7-8

Has there ever been a time in your life when you were so sure of your relationship with God that you felt invincible; there was nothing that would shake your faith? I have. There was a time when I told someone in no uncertain terms, "Oh, I would *never* do that!" Wouldn't you know, it wasn't very long after until the very thing I said I would never do, I did. There's something about our words and actions we should not forget: God hears and sees them all (Psalm 94:9).

Being a believer in Jesus Christ does not take away our humanness. We still make mistakes. So it was with Abram, for right after he believed God about an heir, the Lord said to him, "I am the Lord, who brought you out of Ur of the Chaldeans to give you this land to take possession of it." Abram responded, "Sovereign Lord, how can I know that I will gain possession of it?" (Genesis 15:7-8).

Though Abram was uncertain how God was going to accomplish this promise, the Lord was undeterred. He doesn't change His mind and take away His promise just because we don't understand or we do something wrong. "For the word of the Lord is right and true; he is faithful in all he does" (Psalm 33:4). "The Lord is trustworthy in all he promises and faithful in all he does. The Lord upholds all who fall and lifts up all who are bowed down" (Psalm 145:13-14). This same God tells us in the New Testament "But now he has reconciled you by Christ's physical body through death to present you holy in his sight, without blemish and free from accusation—if you continue in your faith, established and firm, and do not move from the hope held out in the gospel" (Colossians 1:22-23).

Abram had faith, yet he wasn't sure how God was going to fulfill His promise. We too may have doubts and fears that hold us back from receiving all God has for us, but we can be certain of one thing: He is a God who does not lie (Numbers 23:19).

When He tells us we are reconciled to Him by Christ's physical body through death, we can count on it. When He says we are without blemish and free from accusation if we continue in our faith, we can trust He will forgive us when we fall. His ways are so much higher than our ways; His thoughts than our thoughts (Isaiah 55:9). We can trust Him implicitly for He gives us our very breath, and when we call out to Him, He hears our cry and saves us (Psalm 145:19).

Lord, how can I praise You enough, how can I thank You enough, for all Your promises and all Your love toward me? Thank You that, in my humanness, You have made a way to be reconciled to You not only as I walk this earth but forever in eternity. Help me remain faithful by calling upon You in everything I think, do, and say. In Jesus' name, I pray. Amen.

Day 39

The Blood Covenant

Genesis 15:9-21

What I love most about the Bible is its honesty, especially when it comes to the humanness of those that are written about. Abram believed God when He told him his descendants would be like the stars in the sky and God credited it to him as righteousness, but in the very next paragraph when God showed Abram the land his descendants would one day possess, Abram said, "Sovereign Lord, how can I know that I will gain possession of it?" (Genesis 15:8).

God instructed Abram to prepare three animals and cut them in half, along with a dove and pigeon. In those days, a covenant between two people was made by cutting animals in half, then walking between the halves, representing a solemn oath between the two parties that could not be broken. Abram did as the Lord instructed. Then he waited and waited and waited. All day long, nothing happened, except birds of prey came down on the carcasses, and Abram drove them away.

As the sun was setting, Abram fell into a deep sleep and a thick and dreadful darkness came over him. "Then the Lord said to him, 'Know for certain that for four hundred years your descendants will be strangers in a country not their own and that they will be enslaved and mistreated there. But I will punish the nation they serve as slaves, and afterward they will come out with great possessions. You, however, will go to your ancestors in peace and be buried at a good old age. In the fourth generation your descendants will come back here, for the sin of the Amorites has not yet reached its full measure'" (Genesis 15:13-16).

When Abram awoke, a smoking firepot with a blazing torch appeared and passed between the animal halves. "On that day the Lord made a covenant with Abram and said, 'To your descendants I give this land, from the Wadi of Egypt to the great river, the Euphrates...." (Genesis 15:18). When the fire passed between the pieces, this represented the power of God making a covenant with Abram that what He said would one day be fulfilled.

Today, we live in an instant and on-demand society where we think no matter what we want it should be given to us immediately. That is not God's way. He tells us many times throughout Scripture to be patient, and this is what He was saying to Abram, "I am telling you all this, but it will not happen in your lifetime. Now there is a group of people in the land whose behavior has not reached the level of wickedness that the land should be taken from them, but that time will come. Before it does, your descendants will be slaves in a foreign land for four hundred years. It will be a dark and dismal time. They will feel forsaken by Me, but I will hear their cry and deliver them. Then they will inherit the land. This is My solemn oath to you, Abram."

God also made a covenant with us when he sent Jesus to die for our sins; but we must patiently wait for the fulfillment of all He told us will one day come to pass. Jesus will return to this earth, and of His kingdom there will be no end (Isaiah 9:7).

Lord, may I have patience as I await the coming of Your Son, our Savior, Jesus Christ. In Jesus' name, I pray. Amen.

Day 40

Heirs

Genesis 16:1-4

How do you make sense of a forced "love" triangle, especially when one of those involved is a righteous man of God? One way is to possibly justify it by tradition, something which may have been common in Ur of the Chaldeans where Abram and Sarai were originally from. The Book of Jubilees, which is a highly regarded second-century BC Jewish text, yet a pseudepigraphal work—meaning certain of these writings falsely profess to be Biblical in character [1]—records an account of the biblical history of the world from the creation to Moses. There are accounts of worship of false gods, as well as other rituals and practices occurring in the land of Ur.[2] Along with those rituals may have been an accepted practice that men could have children by their slave women if their wife was unable to bear children. If that were true, then Saria's suggestion to Abram that he have sex with her maidservant so she could bear a son would not be unusual. After all, it had been ten years since God promised an heir. Wasn't that long enough to wait?

There is no mention Abram prayed to the Lord before making this decision, but he didn't have to. He already knew the answer. God told him his offspring would be more than the stars in the sky (Genesis 15:5), and he knew that Sarai was his wife; not Hagar.

There are times I read this story and ask, "What was he thinking? God spoke to him directly. Couldn't he have been patient and waited?" But before those words vanish into the night air, I feel a prick in my heart at my own impatience. We have the privilege of knowing how these events unfolded from beginning to end because we have the Bible. Perhaps for Abram, who was the one living life day by day, it was the in-between time from beginning to end that made it so hard to be patient.

Jesus told the apostle John in Revelation 22:12, "Look, I am coming soon! My reward is with me, and I will give to each person according to what they have done." Though we do not know the day or hour of His return (not even Jesus did during His earthly ministry), we can be certain it will happen. But over the almost fifty years of my Christian walk, I have often been impatient, sometimes wondering why it has taken so long and Jesus has not yet returned.

When Paul wrote to the Galatians, he was also writing to us, "Let us not become weary in doing good, for at the proper time we will reap a harvest if we do not give up" (Galatians 6:9).

Despite Abram's act of adultery, God did not withdraw His promise. Though there may be times we sin, He is faithful and just to forgive us our sins (1 John 1:9). He will not withdraw from us His promise of eternity with Him.

While hanging on the cross, Jesus said, "It is finished," which means His purpose for coming was complete. That will never change. Just like God promised Abram an heir, He promises us we too are His heirs if we believe and trust in Him (Galatians 3:29).

Lord, give me the strength and faith to not grow weary but remain faithful to You until the end. In Jesus' name, I pray. Amen.

Day 41

Taking Responsibility

Genesis 16:5-8

Had Abram waited patiently and told Sarai, "God has a different plan," there would have been no adultery and no Ishmael. But like the brilliance of a noonday sun, the light of God's word never sugarcoats the people who are written about. We see them as they are; and, like us, they too have faults.

So Abram had sex with Hagar and she conceived. Something happened, which Sarai was unprepared for: Hagar despised Sarai. Then Sarai said to Abram, "You are responsible for the wrong I am suffering..." (Genesis 16:5). Wow, I bet he didn't see that coming.

He could have said, "It was your idea. Live with it." Instead, he told Sarai, "Do with her whatever you think best" (Genesis 16:6).

Sarai gave her husband an earthly solution to a problem she perceived was causing him grave concern. He took her advice but, when trouble began, he didn't want to deal with it and told Sarai it was her responsibility to take care of it. Sounds like a familiar refrain when we look back to Adam. He not only refused to take responsibility for his actions, he blamed God for "The woman you put here with me" (Genesis 3:12).

When we refuse to take responsibility for our own actions, that is wrong and often causes great suffering for others, as Hagar would soon discover. Sarai treated Hagar so badly that Hagar ran away.

Running away from our problems doesn't solve them; it only compounds them. The more compounded they become, the more our hearts potentially harden toward God (Proverbs 28:13-14). The Lord was not going to allow Abram to pretend he had no responsibility in a situation that was his own doing.

Paul wrote in Colossians 3:25, "Anyone who does wrong will be repaid for their wrongs, and there is no favoritism." However, if we repent and turn to God our sins will be wiped out (Acts 3:19).

Our Lord is a faithful and loving God who wants nothing more than a repentant heart and pure honesty when it comes to taking responsibility for our actions and our sins. And why not? He already knows everything there is to know about us.

Lord, forgive me for ever trying to hide anything from You. Cleanse me and make me whole through the precious blood of Jesus, the One who died for my sins. In Jesus' name, I pray. Amen.

Day 42

The Return

Genesis 16:9-16

What was Hagar thinking as she fled for her life toward Egypt? "How did I get into this mess? It wasn't my idea to sleep with Abram." But here she was alone, frightened, and carrying a married man's child. What was she to do?

Running to the point of exhaustion, she found refreshment at the spring called Beer Lahai Roi, meaning "Well of the Living One who sees me."[1] This is where the angel of the Lord found her, and he said, "Hagar, slave of Sarai, where have you come from, and where are you going?"

The angel did not address Hagar as Abram's wife but as Sarai's slave, an indication of what her position was in this family. Hagar, most likely startled, hot, and dirty, with tears running down her cheeks, answered, "I'm running away from my mistress Sarai" (Genesis 16:8).

With a voice that brought comfort like cool, soothing lotion on dry, cracked skin, the angel told her to, "Go back to your mistress and submit to her…You are now pregnant and you will give birth to a son. You shall name him Ishmael, for the Lord has heard of your misery" (Genesis 16:9 and 11).

Sarai's plan went awry, but God saw Hagar in her place of need and promised if she returned, she and her son would be cared for. Hagar returned and submitted herself to her mistress Sarai, and bore a son. Abram named him Ishmael, of whom the angel told Hagar, "He will be a wild donkey of a man; his hand will be against everyone and everyone's hand against him, and he will live in hostility toward all his brothers" (Genesis 16:12). That does not sound like the son of promise about whom God had spoken to Abram, and he wasn't.

We can learn from this that despite our own failings, God loves us. We may have made many choices ending in bad results—some of our own doing; some because of what others have done. But God can use our life experiences for His purposes when we humble ourselves before Him and do as He directs us to do. Hagar humbled herself before the God who saw her and submitted to Sarai for many years as she raised her son, who would become the father of twelve tribes.

Christianity.com had this to say about Ishmael, "According to biblical tradition and historical interpretations, the descendants of Ishamel are generally considered to be the Arab people. This is based on genealogies and narratives in the Bible and other historical records, suggesting that Ishamel's offspring settled in the Arabian Peninsula."[2] The angel told Hagar, "...he will live in hostility toward all his brothers," and we can see those results taking place even today.

The Lord not only saw Hagar, but He also sees each of us. He knows we make mistakes. He tells us in His Word, "But he gives us more grace. That is why Scripture says: 'God opposes the proud but shows favor to the humble'. . . Humble yourselves before the Lord, and he will lift you up" (James 4:6 and 10).

Lord, thank You for Your plan of salvation through Your Son Jesus Christ, the One who became as one of us, who humbled Himself to the point of death on a cross so that we can be set free from our sins. Humble me in Your presence and make me more like Jesus every day. In Jesus' name, I pray. Amen.

Day 43

Laughter

Genesis 17-18:15

Thirteen years passed. Abram was now ninety-nine years old; Sarai, eighty-nine. We can imagine Abram loved his son Ishmael while Sarai regretted it every day of her life. This is conjecture, but one thing is certain, God was not yet finished with Abram and Sarai. God had something very specific in mind, which so humbled Abram he fell facedown before the Lord. "And God said to him, 'As for me, this is my covenant with you: You will be the father of many nations. No longer will you be called Abram; your name will be Abraham, for I have made you a father of many nations...I will establish my covenant as an everlasting covenant...to be your God and the God of your descendants after you'" (Genesis 17:3-5 and 7).

Similar to marriage, it was a solemn oath, a promise, never meant to be broken. And just like a ring is the symbol of an unending commitment, circumcision of all males eight days and older became the symbol of this covenant between Abraham and God.

"God also said to Abraham, 'As for Sarai your wife, you are no longer to call her Sarai; her name will be Sarah. I will bless her and surely give you a son by her'" (Genesis 17:15-16). At this news, Abraham fell facedown again, but this time he laughed to himself, perhaps thinking God would not hear as he whispered, "Will a son be born to a man a hundred years old? Will Sarah bear a child at the age of ninety?" Then he said to God, "If only Ishmael might live under your blessing" (Genesis 17:17-18).

God told Abraham that Ishmael would be blessed because of him but he was not the heir; that God's everlasting covenant was to be with Isaac (meaning laughter)[1], the son whom Sarah would have a year later. Soon thereafter, three visitors came and confirmed to Abraham that he and Sarah would have a son and name him Isaac. Sarah, who was listening to the conversation, also laughed. At her age, no way!

The Lord heard her laugh, and said, "Is anything too hard for the Lord?" Sarah denied she laughed, but the Lord said to her, "Yes, you did laugh" (Genesis 18:14-15). God hears us and, when He speaks such things as were spoken to Abraham and Sarah, it is nothing to laugh at because it is not in jest (Matthew 12:36-37).

Lord, Your word is so precise in every detail. You knew from the time Adam and Eve sinned that You would choose Abraham to be the father of all nations and the one from whose lineage the Messiah would come. Thank You for Your plan of salvation that is available to everyone who believes. In Jesus' name, I pray. Amen.

Day 44

Intercession

Genesis 18:16-33

When three visitors came to visit Abraham and Sarah, it was a turning point in their relationship with God. Both of them had been given new names, and they were told they would have a son within one year; and God made an everlasting covenant with Abraham.

As the visitors were leaving, something extraordinary occurred. Abraham walked alongside to see them on their way. "Then the Lord said, 'Shall I hide from Abraham what I am about to do? Abraham will surely become a great and powerful nation, and all nations on earth will be blessed through him'" (Genesis 18:17-18).

Abraham apparently did not know where the three were going and what was about to take place as they departed. What I find extraordinary about this is God is debating whether He should reveal to Abraham what is about to happen, and then goes on to describe why, yes, of course, He should. Otherwise, Abraham might think the destruction of Sodom and the surrounding cities was a natural disaster and not an intentional act of judgment because of their wickedness.

"Then the Lord said, 'The outcry against Sodom and Gomorrah is so great and their sin so grievous that I will go down and see if what they have done is as bad as the outcry that has reached me. If not, I will know" (Genesis 18:20-21).

The other two visitors turned away and went toward Sodom, but Abraham remained standing before the Lord. As they stood face to face, Abraham interceded for Sodom and Gomorrah, first asking if the Lord would spare the cities for fifty righteous people, adding, "Far be it from you to do such a thing—to kill the righteous with the wicked. . .Will not the Judge of all the earth do right?"

(Genesis 18:25). When God agreed to spare the cities for the sake of fifty righteous people, Abraham went further, asking for forty-five; then forty; then thirty; then twenty; and then ten. Each time, the Lord responded affirmatively saying He would not destroy the cities if even ten righteous people were found.

Do you find it astonishing that Abraham had boldness to speak with the Creator of the universe in such a way? I do! Yet, because Abraham's relationship with God was so intimate and personal, he did not consider it disrespectful to make this petition.

We, too, can have that kind of relationship with our heavenly Father. How? By believing in Jesus Christ, His Son, who not only died for us but was raised to life. He is the One who has reconciled us to our Father in heaven (2 Corinthians 5:15-20), and He always lives to intercede for us (Hebrews 7:25).

Lord, You who are just yet merciful, thank You for loving me so much that you sent Your Son Jesus, who has reconciled me to You, who now sits at Your right hand and intercedes for me. Thank You for the confidence You have given me to approach Your throne of grace so I can speak with You as did our forefather Abraham. In Jesus' name, I pray. Amen.

Day 45

The Lord, Rich in Love

Genesis 19:1-11

Sodom and Gomorrah, the infamous cities of the plain that most people have heard of but may not know why, were possibly located by the Dead Sea[1]. It was the place where Lot ended up living when he parted ways with his Uncle Abraham.

The two angels arrived at Sodom in the evening, and Lot was sitting in the gateway of the city. Earlier, when they visited Abraham, it was during the heat of the day, in bright sunlight where everything was exposed and open. By the time they arrived in Sodom, it was evening, the time when it is dark and things are hidden.

When Lot saw them coming, he got up and urged them to stay with him and then leave early in the morning, but they answered, "No, we will spend the night in the square" (Genesis 19:2). That might be equivalent to one of us going into an area known for its high crime and setting up camp. Lot wasn't about to let that happen. He insisted strongly that they come with him, and they did.

Before going to bed, loud voices called to Lot, "Where are the men who came to you tonight? Bring them out to us so that we can have sex with them" (Genesis 19:5). Though Lot was horrified, it seems as though the evil in that place dulled his senses, for he offered his two virgin daughters to these men to do what they pleased. That wasn't what the men wanted, and they began moving toward Lot's house to break down the door. The angels grabbed Lot and pulled him back into the house. Then the angels struck the men outside the house with blindness so they could not find the door.

What a terrifying experience this must have been. Apparently, there were not even ten righteous people in that wicked city. The angels then told Lot the cities were about to be destroyed and to get out immediately. It was judgment time, though Lot and his family would be spared if they left as the angels instructed.

There are times in today's world it feels like Sodom and Gomorrah when watching the news or listening to radio. I sometimes wonder why God doesn't do something. Then I read 2 Peter 3:9, which says, "The Lord is not slow in keeping his promise, as some understand slowness. Instead he is patient with you, not wanting anyone to perish, but everyone to come to repentance."

As He did with Sodom, God's judgment is certain to one day come. In the words of King David we are told to "Wait for the Lord; be strong and take heart and wait for the Lord" (Psalm 27:14). "The Lord is gracious and compassionate, slow to anger and rich in love. The Lord is good to all; he has compassion on all he has made" (Psalm 145:8-9). What a merciful and gracious God we serve!

Thank You, Lord, for Your compassion and rich love toward all You have made. Help me be a reflection of who You are so others will see You in me, and desire to have a relationship with You. In Jesus' name, I pray. Amen.

Day 46

The Warning

Genesis 19:12-20

Imagine Lot running frantically through the streets of Sodom, desperate to save his family from the coming destruction. "Son, get ready to leave immediately. The angels who came to see me last night said the city and everyone in it is going to be destroyed. You must leave with us." Then imagine his despair when his sons-in-law looked at him in disbelief as though he were a madman, laughing as if it were a practical joke, then shutting the door in his face (Genesis 19:14).

We live as though this could never happen to us. Yet, in a moment's time, our entire country went on lockdown because of a supposed deadly disease that lurked in unknown places, with the potential to kill millions, and thousands lost their jobs.

If we read our Bibles, we know of another event that will certainly take place at some point in time. It is referred to as "the end times." But when Christians speak about coming judgment, most people shake their heads in disbelief and say it is a joke, or just downright craziness.

Consider what Jesus said in Matthew 24:38-39 and 42 about the end days: "For in the days before the flood, people were eating and drinking, marrying and giving in marriage, up to the day Noah entered the ark; and they knew nothing about what would happen until the flood came and took them all away...Therefore keep watch, because you do not know on what day your Lord will come." That day will come, and once it does there is no turning back. There will be nothing to go back to (2 Peter 2:4-10).

The Lord told Noah of an impending flood. It took 100 years to prepare for the event, giving others time to repent. Lot, too, was given notice, though his was very short. There are other times throughout the Bible when God tells His people what will happen if they do not repent, and gives them ample time to do so. Jesus has given us warning, too, and tells us to keep watch, for we do not know what day He will return to earth. Let's be like the tribe of Issachar, whose 200 chiefs, with all their relatives under their command, understood the times and knew what Israel should do (1 Chronicles 12:32), so that we are not caught off guard!

Lord, since the day I asked Jesus to forgive my sins and come into my life, I have not looked back. I know what I left behind, and I don't want to go back. Help me take hold of that which You promise and be prepared for the day when Jesus will appear in all His glory to set up His kingdom, of which there will be no end. In Jesus' name, I pray. Amen.

Day 47

Faith Versus Fear

Genesis 19:27-38

Smoke from the valley filled the air when fire and brimstone fell on Sodom and Gomorrah. Abraham stood high atop the mountain looking down, not knowing if Lot and his family escaped. Lot did escape, though barely. He went to Zoar. His wife, unfortunately, did not heed God's warning. As they fled the city, she looked back, turned into a pillar of salt and was now gone. Left to raise two daughters on his own, we are not told how Lot was coping, but it seems he may have lost faith in God. He began to fear those around him, leaving Zoar with his daughters to live in a cave.

Though caves are known to have a consistent temperature, they are dark, damp, and not the least bit inviting when it comes to everyday living. Not to excuse their behavior but Lot's daughters must have given up all hope that they would marry and have children. Having grown up in Sodom, who is to say what perversions they were exposed to. They came up with a plan under the guise of preserving their father's lineage.

They must have had some semblance of conscience, though, as they knew their father wouldn't approve so they got him drunk before carrying out their ill-conceived plan. The oldest daughter was the first to have sex with their father after they got him drunk, and then the following night there was a repeat with the youngest. Both became pregnant, and for generations to come the descendants of these two incestuous acts would be a thorn in the side of God's chosen people.[1][2] The oldest daughter's son became the father of what were known as the Moabites; the descendants of the younger daughter's son were known as the Ammonites (Genesis 19:36-38).

Though we may never come up with the sort of plan Lot's daughters did, we say and do things, perhaps only once, that can change the trajectory of our lives far from the plans God has for us. There is a way to avoid such a collision of our faith with fear, and that is by reading God's Word and also being in an attitude of prayer (Philippians 4:6). When we allow each day to fade away without giving an iota of attention to our faith, it begins to drift like smoke from a chimney, ultimately leaving behind a pile of ashes.

You might ask: How do I make time for God when the pressures of life are vying for my attention? The more thought-provoking question might be: How can I cope with the pressures of life without making time for God?

When Jesus said to seek first His kingdom and righteousness, and all these things (what to eat, drink or wear) will be given to you as well, (Matthew 6:33), He wasn't making a suggestion; He was giving a command, and for good reason. It works.

I've heard numerous accounts of God's people being at the brink of disaster, nowhere to turn, not knowing where they would sleep or if they would eat. Because they trusted their Redeemer, He made a way and provided for their need.

I'm not saying we should sit on our backsides all day saying prayers, and then do nothing. It doesn't work that way. We must trust God to guide us by His Spirit, but we also must do our part to make things happen. Had Lot put his faith in God and stayed in Zoar instead of being fearful, the events we just read about may not have taken place.

Lord, help me not to be judge and jury when it comes to Lot and his daughters, but give me the ability to learn from their mistakes. May I be quick to confess my own sins and ask Your forgiveness and mercy. In Jesus' name, I pray. Amen.

DAY 48

INWARD BEAUTY

Genesis 20:1-2

Lately, when I look in the mirror, I see one, two, sometimes even three new wrinkles magically appear on my face and/or neck. I wonder, "How can this be happening? It was only yesterday I was a teenager." Then my mind wanders to the botox and skin cream commercials on TV. I find myself getting sucked into the imaginary world of looking younger no matter my age, quickly waking up to the reality that the models in those ads are maybe thirty years old, if you stretch it. There's no way any of those products is going to make a sixty-something-year-old look thirty again. It just isn't happening!

What's my point? Abraham and Sarah moved on from the place where Abraham had stood before the Lord into the region of the Negev (toward Egypt). They stopped for a while at a place called Gerar where they met Abimelek, its king. Convinced there was no fear of God in this place and that the king would kill him and take his wife, Abraham lied to the king and instructed Sarah to do likewise. Sound familiar? Except this is twenty-five years after telling the same lie to Pharaoh, king of Egypt. You would think Abraham would have learned his lesson, but it seems he lost sight of God and decided to take matters into his own hands again. How easily we revert back to our human ways when we allow our fear to overcome our faith.

Because of this lie, Abimelek took Sarah into his harem. Almost ninety years old at this point, Sarah is getting pretty old, which makes it all the more amazing that this king would find her attractive. But Sarah's beauty and grace did not come from her outward appearance. As Proverbs 31:30 tells us, "Charm is deceptive, and beauty is fleeting; but a woman who fears the Lord is to be praised." In the New Testament, Peter put it so well when he wrote to God's elect, "Your beauty should not come from outward adornment...Rather, it should be that of your inner self, the unfading beauty of a gentle and quiet spirit, which is of great worth in God's sight. For this is the way the holy women of the past who put their hope in God used to adorn themselves. They submitted themselves to their own husbands, like Sarah, who obeyed Abraham and called him her lord" (1 Peter 3:3-6).

The next time I stand in front of a mirror and count my wrinkles, I will think back to Sarah as a reminder that no matter my age, real beauty comes from within, the beauty which reflects the inner peace, humility and love only our Savior can give; an everlasting beauty that does not fade away with age.

Lord, thank You for Your gentle reminder that youth quickly fades and life is but a moment in time. As Paul writes to the Colossians, may we clothe ourselves with compassion, kindness, humility, gentleness and patience, all the virtues that come from within. In Jesus' name, I pray. Amen.

Day 49

Abimelek, Abraham, and Sarah

Genesis 20:3-18

Abimelek realized he had been blind-sided by Abraham and Sarah when God visited him in a dream and said, "You are as good as dead because of the woman you have taken; she is a married woman."

Claiming innocence, Abimelek responded, "Lord, will you destroy an innocent nation? Did he [Abraham] not say to me, 'She is my sister,' and didn't she [Sarah] also say, 'He is my brother'? I have done this with a clear conscience and clean hands."

God's answer was, "Yes, I know you did this with a clear conscience...That is why I did not let you touch her. Now return the man's wife, for he is a prophet, and he will pray for you and you will live" (Genesis 20:3-7).

Here we have a pagan king who in this instance is more righteous than God's prophet Abraham; yet God instructs Abimelek to not only return Sarah to her husband but to ask Abraham to pray for him so that he will live. Abraham must have been pretty embarrassed when Abimelek asked for his prayers. God does have a way of humbling us.

Do you get the impression that even though God is not pleased with Abraham's behavior, Abraham has not lost favor with his Lord? After all, they were in covenant, something which is not to be broken.

Abimelek did what God instructed him to do, but not without giving Abraham a piece of his mind, saying, "What have you done to us? How have I wronged you that you have brought such great guilt upon me and my kingdom? You have done things to me that should never be done. . . What was your reason for doing this?"

Abraham replied, "I said to myself, 'There is surely no fear of God in this place, and they will kill me because of my wife,'" going on to explain how he and Sarah agreed to this deceptive plan.

"Then Abimelek brought sheep and cattle, as well as slaves, and gave them to Abraham. He returned Sarah to him saying, 'My land is before you; live where you like.'"

Abimelek absolved Sarah of any wrong doing, and said to her, "I am giving your brother [Abraham] a thousand shekels of silver. This is to cover the offense against you before all who are with you; you are completely vindicated."

Then Abraham prayed to God, and God healed Abimelek, his wife and his slave girls so they could have children again, for the Lord had closed up every womb in Abimelek's household because of Abraham's wife Sarah (Genesis 20:9-18).

Before this incident, God spoke to Abraham and Sarah that within the year they would have an heir, the son of promise. Although they knew this, they seemingly fell for a trap of Satan, which I believe one can surmise was to thwart God's plan. As long as she was in Abimelek's harem, Abraham and Sarah were separated. How then was this son to be born? But God spoke, and His authority prevailed.

It's comforting to know God does not forsake His children when they fail Him. It took a pagan king to remind Abraham of that. Let's pray our dedication to Jesus is so cemented in His Word and in our personal relationship with Him, that we won't need an unbeliever to remind us of our commitment to serve our Lord and King.

Heavenly Father, thank You for Your not-so-subtle reminder of what can happen when I take my eyes off of You. Help me keep my commitment to You daily by reading Your Word and being in prayer. Help me also to remember that my struggle is not against flesh and blood but against an enemy who is always looking for ways to embarrass and shame me. May I clothe myself with the armor of Your protection which You have so generously given me to put on. In Jesus' name, I pray. Amen.

Day 50

God is Never in a Hurry

Genesis 21:1-7

Almost twenty-five years after God told Abraham his descendants would be like the stars in the sky, too numerous to count, Isaac, the son of promise, was born. It's pretty obvious God is never in a hurry; in contrast to us who are often in a hurry. "Now the Lord was gracious to Sarah as he had said, and the Lord did for Sarah what he had promised. Sarah became pregnant and bore a son to Abraham in his old age, at the very time God had promised him" (Genesis 21:1-2). Sarah's laughter, which once came because of unbelief, was now laughter of sheer joy as she held her precious son in her arms, giving thanks to God for keeping His promise in their old age.In these two sentences we learn that God is gracious and He keeps His promises. Are those not the virtues we look for in others, but rarely find? How glorious that we can be in relationship with the God of the universe who is gracious and keeps His promises. When He told Abraham and Sarah they would have a son and when he would arrive, it happened just as He said.

There are also Old Testament Scriptures foretelling the birth of another son, God's very own. He said this Son will come again, that the government will be on his shoulders, and "Of the greatness of his government and peace there will be no end" (Isaiah 9:6-7). We can know with certainty this too will come to pass, for God has a 100% track record of keeping His word. There have been numerous times when my prayers seem to go unanswered, and I grow impatient. But when I sit in the solitude of His presence and read what is written in His Word, knowing His promises are true, I become more willing to wait patiently for His answers. God's timing is always perfect. We can count on it.

Thank You, Lord, for yet another lesson on how gracious, loving, and kind You are toward me. Help me when my impatience interferes with what You know is best. Fill me with the wonder and awe of Your Spirit, knowing You hear my prayers and You will answer in Your perfect timing. In Jesus, name, I pray. Amen.

Day 51

Born of the Flesh or of the Spirit?

Genesis 21:8-21

Abraham held a great feast when Isaac was weaned, but not everyone was celebrating. Sarah witnessed Ishmael mocking his little brother Isaac, alarming her enough to possibly fear for his safety. She went to Abraham and insisted that he not only send Ishmael away, but also Hagar. Abraham was distressed by this, "But God said to him, 'Do not be so distressed about the boy and your slave woman. Listen to whatever Sarah tells you, because it is through Isaac that your offspring will be reckoned'" (Genesis 21:12).

Isaac, a type of Christ in some ways, was chosen to be the heir of God's promise to Abraham. It was time for him to take his rightful place in the family.

"Early the next morning Abraham took some food and a skin of water and gave them to Hagar. He set them on her shoulders and then sent her off with the boy. She went her way and wandered in the Desert of Beersheba" (Genesis 21:14).

It was a difficult journey through the desert. Hagar thought they were both going to die. God said to her, "Lift the boy up and take him by the hand, for I will make him into a great nation."

"Then God opened her eyes and she saw a well of water. So she went and filled the skin with water and gave the boy a drink. God was with the boy as he grew up" (Genesis 21:18-20).

Ishmael and Isaac represent a deep divide in the human race. What is this divide between two sons? The late David Pawson, author of *Unlocking the Bible,* explains it this way, "It is the division between Israeli and Arab. That is a bad enough division, but that is not the deepest gulf in the human race. It is the division between Jew and Gentile. That, too, is not the deepest division between the human race. It is basically the division between those who are born of the flesh and those who are born of the spirit. There is no deeper division than that. It cuts the human race right in two, and everybody is either an Ishmael, born of the flesh, or an Isaac, born of the Spirit."[1]

We are all born an Ishmael. It isn't until we ask Jesus Christ to come into our lives that we become an Isaac. This is our choice: Will we remain in the flesh to which we were born, and die in our sins? Or will we be born of the Spirit, and live for Christ?

We can live for ourselves, doing all the things we think necessary to obtain favor with God: doing good, being kind, thereby trying to make our own way to heaven; or we can live for God and, as Paul says, "that those who live should no longer live for themselves but for him [Jesus] who died for them and was raised again" (2 Corinthians 5:15).

Do we want to be sons and daughters born by the slave woman (Hagar) in the ordinary way, and always remain there? Or do we want to be sons and daughters by the free woman (Sarah) who are born as the result of promise (Galatians 4:21-31)? As followers of Jesus Christ, our answer should be evident.

Lord, help me understand fully the difference between flesh and spirit, slavery and freedom. Help me always make the choice that honors You and sets me free to be all You want me to be. In Jesus' name, I pray. Amen.

Day 52

Trust

Genesis 21:22-34

I once read a book titled *Trust* by Marie Timm. It's the true story of an abused horse that came into Marie's life. After many years of overwhelming dedication and hard work, Marie gained the trust of Paladin, and they became the best of friends.

"It was just a horse," you might say. Yes, but I believe animals have inherent instincts that God has put there for a reason, and this animal knew it would be a long time before it could or would trust a human being to care for it again, if ever.

Human beings also have instincts. Once we've been betrayed, it is nearly impossible to again trust the betrayer; that is, unless God is in the mix. So, when Abraham was approached by Abimelek to enter into a treaty, Abimelek had to be certain he could trust Abraham to keep his end of the bargain. After all, Abraham had lied to him about Sarah being his wife, which brought a pretty serious curse on Abimelek's household (Genesis 20:17-18).

When Abimelek and his commander came to Abraham, he said, "God is with you in everything you do. Now swear to me here before God that you will not deal falsely with me or my children or my descendants. Show to me and the country where you now reside as a foreigner the same kindness I have shown you." Based on their previous encounter, Abimelek knew Abraham was a man of God. Apparently, because of this, he wanted to align himself with Abraham and receive not only a blessing but protection in the event he and his country needed help. Abraham agreed, and responded, "I swear it" (Genesis 21:22-24).

Before Abraham agreed to this treaty, he wanted to rectify an issue concerning a well that had been taken by some of Abimelek's servants. "But Abimelek said, 'I don't know who has done this. You did not tell me, and I heard about it only today'" (Genesis 21:26).

Trust having been restored, the two men made a treaty. The issue of the well was then resolved at Beersheba, meaning "the well of the oath."[1] After Abimelek and his commander returned to the land of the Philistines, "Abraham planted a tamarisk tree in Beersheba, and there he called on the name of the Lord, the Eternal God. And Abraham stayed in the land of the Philistines for a long time" (Genesis 21:33-34).

This must have been a place of solace where Abraham could commune with God and God with him, something which he most certainly needed for what was about to happen next in his life.

Lord, it's difficult to trust others when they have betrayed me. Forgive me for the times I have also betrayed the trust of someone, and help me make it right. I'm thankful You are trustworthy, that what You say is always true. Thank You for this assurance. Help me look to You as my source of strength so that I, too, will be a reflection of who You are, and be the person others can trust. In Jesus' name, I pray. Amen.

DAY 53

TWO SACRIFICES

Genesis 22:1-12

"Then God said [to Abraham], 'Take your son, your only son, whom you love—Isaac—and go to the region of Moriah. Sacrifice him there as a burnt offering on a mountain I will show you'" (Genesis 22:2).

Imagine God asking you to do this. What would your response be? Mine might be, "Have you lost your mind, Lord?"

Not Abraham. He got up early the next morning, saddled his donkey, took two servants, and his son Isaac, as well as the wood for the burnt offering.

God did not ask Abraham to do something He Himself would not do. Though it would be thousands of years later, He too "gave his one and only Son, that whoever believes in him shall not perish but have eternal life" (John 3:16).

Just as "On the third day, Abraham looked up and saw the place in the distance" (Genesis 22:4), Jesus was raised from the dead on the third day (Acts 10:40).

Abraham instructed his servants to stay with the donkey, and said that only he and Isaac would go to worship, and then come back (Genesis 22:5). Jesus went to the Garden of Gethsemane to be alone with His Father (Luke 22:39-44).

On their way, Isaac asked his father about the sacrifice. "Abraham answered, 'God Himself will provide the lamb'" (Genesis 22:8). Jesus is the Lamb of God who takes away the sins of the world (John 1:29).

When they reached the place of sacrifice, Abraham built the altar, then bound his son and laid him on it. He then reached up and took the knife to slay him. Isaac never said a word (Genesis 22:9). When taken before Pilate and accused, "Jesus still made no reply, and Pilate was amazed" (Mark 15:5).

"The angel of the Lord called out to him from heaven, 'Abraham! Abraham! ... do not lay a hand on the boy...Now I know that you fear God, because you have not withheld from me your son, your only son.' Abraham looked up and there in a thicket he saw a ram caught by its horns. He went over and took the ram and sacrificed it as a burnt offering instead of his son" (Genesis 22:11-13).

Abraham's faith in God was so strong, he was willing to sacrifice Isaac, "even though God had said to him, 'It is through Isaac that your offspring will be reckoned.' Abraham reasoned that God could even raise the dead, and so in a manner of speaking he did receive Isaac back from death" (Hebrews 11:18-19).

Scripture does not elaborate on how Isaac coped with these events as they unfolded, except when he asked Abraham where the sacrifice was. It appears as though he knew, and was willing to trust his father without question.

So it was with Jesus, who said, "The reason my Father loves me is that I lay down my life—only to take it up again. No one takes it from me, but I lay it down of my own accord. I have authority to lay it down and authority to take it up again. This command I received from my Father" (John 10:17-18).

Abraham proved his faithfulness to God, and his son was saved. God's faithfulness through sacrificing His only Son saves us from our sins, and offers us an eternity in heaven with Him.

What an amazing story of Abraham's love for God, and of God's love for us. May this truth penetrate deep into our souls so that we might grasp how wide and long and high and deep is the love of Christ, and to know His love that surpasses knowledge (Ephesians 3:18-19).

Lord Jesus, thank You for Your faithfulness in dying on a cross and shedding Your blood for my sins. It is beyond understanding to realize You love me this much. Fill me each day with the power of Your Spirit, giving me a greater understanding of this unsurpassing love that belongs to all who call upon Your name. In Jesus' name, I pray. Amen.

Day 54

God's Reward for Faithfulness

Genesis 22:13-24

"The angel of the Lord called to Abraham from heaven a second time and said, 'I swear by myself, declares the Lord, that because you have done this and have not withheld your son, your only son, I will surely bless you and make your descendants as numerous as the stars in the sky and as the sand on the seashore. Your descendants will take possession of the cities of their enemies, and through your offspring all nations on earth will be blessed, because you have obeyed me" (Genesis 22:15-18). These words, "because you have obeyed me," should remind us of the importance of obedience in order to receive God's blessing.

There is no mention of the emotional turmoil Abraham might have experienced through all of this. It's not beyond our imagination to believe he struggled. The glorious thing is, he endured the test without complaint, and his reward was immeasurable. His son was restored to him. Little could he know that thousands of years later, his descendant Jesus would also be restored to His heavenly Father after sacrificing Himself on the cross for our sins (Hebrews 1:3).

As we continue to the end of this chapter, verses 20-24 may seem somewhat out of place. It is important, though, to know who people are. This may be the reason we are now introduced to Nahor, Abraham's brother. Nahor's wife Milcah had a son named Bethuel, the father of Rebekah, who became Isaac's wife.

Abraham's obedience and faithfulness made it possible for his son Isaac to carry the mantle of the covenant made between God and Abraham. May we too be faithful, without complaint, especially when we walk through dark times. May we trust God to bring us through, knowing our reward will be great. It may not happen until eternity, but we can rest assured it will indeed happen.

Lord, I pray that no matter the heartache, no matter the struggle, I will remain faithful to You, without complaint and without worry. Help me trust that through the darkness You are my light that always shines and points the way. I ask for Your endurance and patience so I may joyfully give thanks to You, the One who has qualified me to share in the inheritance of the saints in the kingdom of light (Colossians 1:11-12). In Jesus' name, I pray. Amen.

Day 55

The Death of Sarah

Genesis 23

If anyone could run out of patience with God, it would have been Abraham. God told him he would inherit the land he was now a stranger and sojourner in, but he had not one piece of property to his name. God also told him he would be unable to count his descendants; yet his son was almost 40 years old, unmarried, and there were no grandchildren. Then Sarah, who had been with Abraham throughout this entire journey, who had been a caring wife and mother, died at the age of 127. It was a great loss to Abraham, who mourned and wept over her. He did not mourn and weep endlessly, though, for he had faith she was with God.

Death is not something we should ever fear, for this is not our permanent dwelling place. Instead, we are looking for the enduring city that is to come (Hebrews 13:14). In speaking to the disciples, Jesus said, "Very truly I tell you, whoever hears my word and believes him who sent me has eternal life and will not be judged but has crossed over from death to life" (John 5:24). Though it is proper and even expected to mourn and weep when we lose loved ones, we should not stay there. I love what Matthew Henry said about what we should say in reaction to loved ones who have gone to be with the Lord: "We are going."[1]

Because Abraham owned no land, he wasn't certain where to bury Sarah. He went to the Hittites, who were among those who owned and occupied the land, and said, "I am a foreigner and stranger among you. Sell me some property for a burial site here so I can bury my dead" (Genesis 23:4). The Hittites knew Abraham was a foreigner, and they weren't certain they wanted to sell him any land. They hesitated, offering to give him their fields to use so he could bury Sarah on their land. Abraham insisted, and Ephron, the Hittite, said, "Listen to me, my lord; the land is worth four hundred shekels of silver, but what is that between you and me? Bury your dead" (Genesis 23:14-15). In other words, if you want to pay this price, you can have the land.

They agreed, and the land "was deeded to Abraham as his property in the presence of all the Hittites who had come to the gate of the city" (Genesis 23:17-18).

It took the death of Abraham's wife to see the beginning of God's promise to him. He finally owned a small piece of the Promised Land.[2]

Lord, thank You for Abraham's life and his example of true faith. In difficult times of loss, help me never forget that this earth is, indeed, not my permanent home. You have prepared a place for me that I cannot even imagine. May the eyes of my heart be enlightened so that I may know the hope to which You have called me, the riches of Your glorious inheritance in Your holy people, and Your incomparably great power for those who believe (Ephesians 1:18). In Jesus' name, I pray. Amen.

Day 56

A Solemn Oath

Genesis 24:1-9

With the death of Sarah, Abraham's focus turned to finding a wife for his son Isaac, who at the age of forty didn't seem in any hurry to get married. But Abraham did not want just any wife for his son. He wanted someone who had the same values and beliefs in God as he did. That did not include the women of Canaan, the land where they were living and the land which God had promised would one day belong to Abraham's descendants. Abraham enlisted his chief household servant, presumably Eliezer, to carry out this task.

Why Abraham didn't send his son or go himself, we don't know. Maybe he was too old and unable to make such a trip, or perhaps it was because he knew if he left he and/or his son might not want to return to the Promised Land. He'd been distracted before, so this might have been a possibility.

Before sending his servant on this journey, Abraham said to him, "Put your hand under my thigh." Searching for material on the significance of such an oath, several sources indicate this was the closest place to the genitals, and that "Abraham had been promised a 'seed' by God, and this covenantal blessing was passed on to his son and grandson."[1]

Keil and Blitz *Biblical Commentary on the Old Testament* states: "The oath was by 'Jehovah, God of heaven and earth,' as the God who rules in heaven and on earth, not by Elohim; for it had respect not to an ordinary oath, but to a question of great importance in relation to the kingdom of God. Isaac was not regarded as a merely pious candidate for matrimony, but as the heir of the promise."[2]

Abraham continued with further instruction to his servant, "I want you to swear by the Lord, the God of heaven and the God of earth, that you will not get a wife for my son from the daughters of the Canaanites, among whom I am living, but you will go to my country and my own relatives and get a wife for my son Isaac."

"The servant asked him, 'What if the woman is unwilling to come back with me to this land? Shall I then take your son back to the country you came from?'" Abraham's answer was a resounding, "No."

"Abraham said, 'The Lord, the God of heaven, who brought me out of my father's household and my native land and who spoke to me and promised me on oath, saying, "To your offspring I will give this land"—he will send his angel before you so that you can get a wife for my son from there. If the woman is unwilling to come back with you, then you will be released from this oath of mine. Only do not take my son back there.' So the servant put his hand under the thigh of his master Abraham and swore an oath to him concerning this matter" (Genesis 24:3-9).

This event represents the seriousness of taking an oath. It meant you were true to your word, and you would do as you swore to do.

In times past, when a witness came to testify in court, he swore an oath on the Holy Bible to tell the truth. This meant that what came out of the witness' mouth would be heard not only by those in the courtroom but by God; therefore, it would be the truth. Nowadays, a witness takes an oath to tell the truth but not by any standard to which they are held accountable, except maybe being fined or put in jail if they are found to have lied. It no longer has the same effect as swearing before the God of heaven and earth (Hebrews 6:16).

As Christians, we are admonished, even without taking an oath, "Do not lie to each other, since you have taken off your old self with its practices and have put on the new self, which is being renewed in knowledge in the image of its Creator" (Colossians 3:9-10). Our word to our spouse, children, friends, and colleagues should always be the truth. When we say we will do something, we need to do it. This not only shows that we keep our promises, but gives glory and honor to our Lord.

Thank You, Father, for giving me instruction on the importance of keeping my word, not only to my loved ones, friends, and acquaintances but to You. Keep me ever mindful that when I asked Jesus to be Lord and Savior of my life, I committed to a lifetime of service and honor to You. Help me to be a person who does not lie and who keeps my word, so You will be glorified. In Jesus' name, I pray. Amen.

Day 57

Answered Prayer

Genesis 24:10-27

Abraham's servant made preparations for his long journey by taking camels, as well as jewelry, clothing, and other costly gifts. He was determined to carry out his oath for Abraham. When he arrived in Nahor, the land of Abraham's family, it was evening, the time women came to draw water.

The first thing he did was pray a very specific prayer. He wanted an answer from God. "See, I am standing beside this spring, and the daughters of the townspeople are coming out to draw water. May it be that when I say to a young woman, 'Please let down your jar that I may have a drink,' and she says, 'Drink, and I'll water your camels too'—let her be the one you have chosen for your servant Isaac. By this I will know that you have shown kindness to my master" (Genesis 24:13-14).

Almost before he finished praying, Rebekah came out with her jar on her shoulder. When Abraham's servant asked her for some water, she quickly lowered the jar to her hands and gave him to drink. Then she offered to draw water for his camels.

Do you think he was having difficulty containing his excitement at this point? It is a beautiful thing when we pray and God sends an instant answer. It doesn't always happen that way, but what a blessing when it does.

Abraham's servant gives us a great lesson about being tactful. He doesn't immediately blurt out why he is there. He asks a favor of Rebekah, a drink of water, which begins a conversation between them.

I sometimes criticize myself that I have not knowingly led anyone to Christ, especially when I read and hear about those who have. I have learned it is not always about approaching someone the first time you meet and asking, "Are you saved?" Sometimes it takes getting to know a person and building a relationship of trust, allowing the Holy Spirit to work and produce the fruit. We may not know this side of heaven who will be there because of our kindness and words of comfort toward them.

Paul wrote to the Corinthians about this very thing when he said, "I planted the seed, Apollos watered it, but God has been making it grow. So neither the one who plants nor the one who waters is anything, but only God, who makes things grow" (1 Corinthians 3:6-7).

"Then [Abraham's servant] asked, 'Whose daughter are you? Please tell me, is there room in your father's house for us to spend the night?'

"She answered him, 'I am the daughter of Bethuel, the son that Milkah bore to Nahor.'" Remember Genesis 22:20-24?

"And she added, 'We have plenty of straw and fodder, as well as room for you to spend the night.' Then the man bowed down and worshiped the Lord saying, 'Praise be to the Lord, the God of my master Abraham...As for me, the Lord has led me on the journey to the house of my master's relatives'" (Genesis 24:23-27).

What an example of a godly man who not only prayed before taking any action, but when his prayer was answered he immediately bowed down and worshiped the Lord, giving Him thanks and praise.

There are many Scriptures in the Bible that speak to the importance of prayer. It would take multiple pages to mention them. Prayer in the life of a Christian is so important that Jesus told His disciples a parable to show them they should always pray and not give up (Luke 18:1). The apostle Paul wrote to the Philippians about this saying, "Do not be anxious about anything, but in every situation, by prayer and petition, with thanksgiving, present your requests to God" (Philippians 4:6). It's important to remember to give thanks when we receive the answer to our prayers, for the Lord is good.

Heavenly Father, I rejoice in Your goodness. Thank You that when I pray, You hear my prayers. May I always trust that even when the answers don't come immediately or in the way I think they should, You are faithful. In Jesus' name, I pray. Amen.

Day 58

Rebekah's Answer

Genesis 24:28-58

What began as an ordinary day for Rebekah ended in a life-changing decision. Imagine the emotions she experienced when a perfect stranger asked her for a drink of water, then told her she had been chosen by God to be the wife of his master's son. And he knew this because of the prayer he just prayed. Would your reaction be like that of Rebekah's? I'm not sure mine would have been!

Rebekah was so thrilled by what this man said, she ran home and told everyone. Her brother hurried out to meet Abraham's servant, and said, "Why are standing out here? I have prepared the house and a place for the camels" (Genesis 24:31). Then they went into the house and offered him food, but he refused to eat until he explained why he was there.

The atmosphere in that home would have been electrifying as the servant spoke of his mission and how God answered his prayer. "Laban [Rebekah's brother] and Bethuel [her father] answered, 'This is from the Lord; we can say nothing to you one way or the other. Here is Rebekah; take her and go, and let her become the wife of your master's son, as the Lord has directed.' When Abraham's servant heard what they said, he bowed down to the ground before the Lord" (Genesis 24:50-52). It's noteworthy that the Lord is mentioned in every decision by all involved.

Abraham's servant then blessed Rebekah and her family with the gifts he brought. That evening they ate and drank together in a festive celebration. Abraham's servant spent the night, but the next morning it was back to business when he said, "Send me on my way to my master." Rebekah's family hesitated. They weren't sure they wanted her to leave so suddenly, and they asked that she be allowed to remain for ten days. But Abraham's servant insisted, "Do not detain me, now that the Lord has granted success to my journey. Send me on my way so I may go to my master." They were still hesitant, and responded, "Let's call the young woman and ask her about it." When they asked her, she said, "I will go" (Genesis 24:53-58).

It was a drastic change for this family, but Rebekah knew she was chosen by God. Her quick response is beautiful. It's an example we should follow when we know God has a calling on our life. There is no time to hesitate. If we do, the opportunity may be lost. Had Rebekah decided to stay with her family those ten days, who knows what might have happened. We don't have to wonder, though, because she did exactly as the Lord directed her. She went, and she was blessed for it.

Lord God Almighty, thank You for the lives of those who came before us, who through their actions have shown what it means to be obedient. They were far from perfect, just as we are, but when they answered You, You blessed them. Help me learn from them and know that when I do not hesitate, You are always faithful in fulfilling Your purpose for my life. In Jesus' name, I pray. Amen.

Day 59

Isaac and Rebekah

Genesis 24:59-67

What was Isaac thinking during this time? He surely knew his father sent his servant to find a wife. Was he anxious, impatient, worried? We read in Scripture that he was out in the field near his home one evening meditating. That's a serene picture of a man who knows God has everything under control. We're not told what his prayer was, but during this quiet time with God he looked up and saw camels approaching.

"Rebekah also looked up and saw Isaac. She got down from her camel and asked the servant, 'Who is that man in the field coming to meet us?'

"'He is my master,' the servant answered. So she took her veil and covered herself. Then the servant told Isaac all he had done. Isaac brought her into the tent of his mother Sarah, and he married Rebekah" (Genesis 24:64-67).

How old-fashioned, you might say. Or you might think: *They didn't even know each other yet; how could they do that? What, no engagement?* Before judging history by today's standards, arranged marriages were not unusual during that time. This marriage was very different, though, as it was a marriage arranged by God. It was holy, it was ordained, and it was to fulfill His plan and purpose, not theirs. The romantic and touching part about this "arranged marriage" by God is that we are told, "So she became his wife, and he loved her" (Genesis 24:67).

Oh, they would have their challenges, but what marriage doesn't? This is why it is important to marry a believer in Christ Jesus so that when challenges come, we have Jesus to go to together for help. Marriage is a sacred commitment not to be taken lightly. It should be honored by all and the marriage bed kept pure (Hebrews 13:4). "Didn't the Lord make you one with your wife? In body and spirit you are his. And what does he want? Godly children from your union. So guard your heart; remain loyal to the wife of your youth. 'For I hate divorce!' says the Lord, the God of Israel" (Malachi 2:15-16, NLT).

Lord, for those of us who are older and have perhaps been married for a while, this may not seem like such an issue, but for young people in today's society, it certainly is. They are bombarded with many confusing ideas in the world about their sexuality. I know Your Word leaves no question as to who we are in You. I pray right now, especially for those who are young and contemplating marriage, that they not only seek advice from godly people who are already married, but that they seek Your desire for their lives. I pray they find the partner best suited for them, and so honor You as a witness to what a godly marriage can truly be. In Jesus' name, I pray. Amen.

Day 60

A Divine Pattern

Genesis 24

After listening to sermons, doing research, and being in prayer, I believe this is the appropriate place to expand, in my own words, on the sermon, "A Divine Pattern," preached by the late David Pawson.[1] Though this sermon dates back to the late 1960s, it is still applicable to today. What a testimony to the Scripture which says God never changes (Malachi 3:6).

A pattern is where it all begins when it comes to sewing, and that's how I think of this. We take the pieces of a pattern and lay them on fabric. We cut the fabric, and then sew the pieces together to give us a finished product. In this instance, God is the creator of the pattern; Abraham, Abraham's servant, and Isaac and Rebekah are the fabric. The finished product is the knowledge we have that God worked everything out by His divine pattern, and for His intended purpose.

Isaac is a pattern of Christ. As he and his father Abraham were walking towards the place of sacrifice (think of Calvary), he most likely helped carry the wood (think of the cross of Jesus), which was to be used in the process of his death. And though Isaac was rescued from this fate seconds before the knife came down, we mustn't forget Abraham who represents a pattern of God because he was willing to sacrifice the son of promise. We know God did this for us (1 John 4:9-10), and that Jesus willingly laid down his life for us (1 John 3:16).

Then we have Abraham (God's representative), who sent his servant (the Holy Spirit), on behalf of Isaac (Christ), to find Rebekah (the bride of Christ). The analogy of each person in the natural to their spiritual counterpart demonstrates how things that take place in the spiritual realm can come to fruition in the natural realm.

Lord, what a beautiful example of who You are as we read about the lives of Abraham, Abraham's servant, and Isaac and Rebekah. Thank You that You have not left me alone with no guidance for how to live for You. May I never take the Bible for granted. Help me not make excuses, but to read it every day. May the words of my mouth and the meditations of my heart be pleasing in Your sight, drawing me ever closer to You. In Jesus' name, I pray. Amen.

Day 61

The Death of Abraham

Genesis 25:1-18

Some portions of the Bible leave us with more questions than answers. Abraham's marriage to Keturah might be one of those portions. We know little, if anything, about Keturah, except that she bore Abraham six children. It's unclear as to whether this marriage took place before or after Sarah died. Some scholars believe it was before, some after. Because of the many opinions on this subject, I will simply say I don't know. I do know there are many examples throughout the Old Testament of men having both wives and concubines, and in 1 Chronicles 1:32, Keturah is referred to as Abraham's concubine. This could mean she was a part of his life when Sarah was alive, and the children were born during that time. Since the Bible doesn't elaborate, we don't know and will have to leave it at that.

Though I firmly believe God's plan for marriage is one man and one woman, in Abraham's case God does not condone nor condemn Abraham's choice to father children by more than one wife. What we do know is that Isaac is the son of promise, and the one through whom eventually came the Savior of the world.

Abraham died at the age of 175, an old man "full of years." He lived a life of promise and purpose because he had faith in the one true God. Ishmael and Isaac buried their father in the field of Ephron, which Abraham had bought to bury his wife, Sarah.

Ishmael is mentioned in this chapter, as are his twelve sons who were tribal rulers according to their settlements and camps. Other than saying they lived in hostility toward all their brothers, there is not much said as to who they are, and where exactly they ended up living. Muslims believe Ishmael was a prophet and an ancestor of Muhammad.[1] Many Arabs also believe they are Ishmael's descendants, which if true, could explain why they live in hostility toward their brothers. That's the scenario we find ourselves in today: conflict between the Jews and Arabs. Whoever these descendants were and are, the Bible says nothing about any of their accomplishments. It apparently was not worth noting when it came to God's story, for they neither believed in nor served Him.

Before he died, Abraham left everything to Isaac, though he also gave gifts to the sons of his concubine, sending them away from his son Isaac to the land of the east, leaving little chance that they would be able to lay claim to any of Isaac's inheritance. Abraham knew Isaac was the son of promise. He blessed him as such, and made him heir of his entire estate, including the Promised Land which didn't yet belong to him.

This part of the story may not apply much to us today other than as historical information about the latter years of Abraham, his sons, and his death. We know Abraham was a man of God who at the end of his life knew Isaac was the chosen one of God, and he gave him everything. We also know that a life such as Ishmael's and his sons, despite possible wealth and accomplishments, did not gain favor with God.

So, the question again arises: Are we an Isaac or an Ishmael; a person of faith or a person of the world?

Lord, I have come to passages in Your Word that seem so far removed from me, it's difficult to understand their significance to my life today. I trust they serve a purpose for teaching, rebuking, correcting, and training in righteousness so that I may be thoroughly equipped for every good work (2 Timothy 3:16), and I thank You for this. In Jesus' name, I pray. Amen.

Day 62
Deceit and Lies; Promises and Blessings

The next several chapters of Genesis reflect a continuing theme of deception, a problem we still struggle with today. Let's pause and consider our own experiences. Have you ever lied about something and then tried to cover it up by telling another lie, and then another lie? I vividly remember a time when I was a teenager and told my mother a lie. I had begged her to go to a movie with a boyfriend. She finally relented and, against her better judgment, let me go. My boyfriend and I decided to meet some friends at a pool hall instead. We never made it to the movie. When I got home, mom asked, "How was the movie?"

"Oh, it was okay. We had fun."

Not knowing she'd seen the movie I told her we were going to, she asked, "What did you like best?"

I had seen some previews so I said something about a part I had seen, told her I was tired and wanted to go to bed. She didn't say anything else until later when she came to my room and asked, "What did you really do tonight?"

My mind went sort of haywire because I thought she had believed me, and I was trying to think of another "believable" lie to tell her. Instead, I decided to tell the truth. It felt like a weight lifted off my chest because even though I knew there would be consequences, I couldn't deal with lying about something I had no reason to lie about. When I told her, she wasn't as upset about where I had been as the fact I had lied to her. That was a life lesson I've never forgotten, which leads me to the life of Isaac.

Chapters 25-28 of Genesis continue the story of four people: Isaac, Rebekah, and their twin sons, Esau and Jacob. It's full of promises, prayers, blessings, stealing, deceit, and lying. Despite the good, the bad, the failings, and the weaknesses, God accomplished His plans. As we will see along this journey, a great nation was born of Abraham, and they are still with us to this day.

What can we learn from this? What I've learned is that it's better to be honest. But when we do mess up, we can trust the Lord to not only forgive us but help us do better. Just like my mom didn't stop loving me because I lied to her, the Lord never stops loving us (1 Chronicles 16:34).

Heavenly Father, I'm so thankful for Your Word, which says that an honest witness tells the truth, but a false witness tells lies (Proverbs 12:17). I pray for strength and wisdom to never lie and to make the right choices that always honor You. In Jesus' name, I pray. Amen.

Day 63

Esau and Jacob

Genesis 25:19-26

The lives of Isaac and Rebekah echo a familiar refrain. After almost twenty years of marriage, they had no children. Isaac prayed to the Lord on behalf of his wife because she couldn't have children, and the Lord answered his prayer. His wife Rebekah became pregnant. There's no mention of Isaac having concubines or other children, which makes for a lot less family drama, at least until the children are grown.

Isaac is a man of prayer who cares deeply about his wife, and so he prays to God for her. Imagine if husbands consistently prayed for their wives when they had a need, or even when they didn't. The need may not be for a child, but a husband should have such an intimate relationship with his wife that he knows how to pray for her.

Peter, the only disciple we know of who was married, wrote: "In the same way, you husbands must give honor to your wives. Treat your wife with understanding as you live together. She may be weaker than you are, but she is your equal partner in God's gift of new life. Treat her as you should so your prayers will not be hindered" (1 Peter 3:7, NLT).

Rebekah's pregnancy wasn't easy as the two babies jostled each other within her. She was so concerned about this, she inquired of the Lord, "Why is this happening to me?" (Genesis 25:22). It's always a good thing to go to the Lord when we are struggling with something.

"The Lord said to her, 'Two nations are in your womb, and two peoples from within you will be separated; one people will be stronger than the other, and the older will serve the younger'" (Genesis 25:23).

Rebekah received her answer, although she may not have fully understood its implications at the time. The two not only became nations, but they came to represent something even deeper than that. Esau represents the human nature and the world[1]; Jacob, after he truly turned his life to God, represents the Spirit of God and His kingdom[2].

Esau became a skillful hunter, a man of the open country, while Jacob was a quiet man, staying among the tents. Isaac, who had a taste for wild game, loved Esau, but Rebekah loved Jacob. This statement is telling in that it may be one, among many reasons, for the sibling rivalry between Esau and Jacob. They were so different from each other, it's hard to imagine they were twins, and each parent loved one of them more than the other.

As the oldest of six children, I can speak from experience that it's best for parents not to show favoritism. It's difficult enough to get a parent's love and affection with that many children, but it can definitely create jealousy and hard feelings if one child feels less loved than another.

It seems as though the lives of these two brothers were on opposite paths, which makes me wonder if they even had affection for one another. Esau was gone a lot of the time; Jacob stayed close to home. On one occasion when Jacob cooked some stew, Esau came in from the open country. "He said to Jacob, 'Quick, let me have some of that red stew! I'm famished!' Jacob replied, 'First sell me your birthright.' 'Look, I am about to die,' Esau said. 'What good is the birthright to me?'" But before Jacob gave his brother stew, he made him swear an oath that he would sell his birthright. So, for some bread and lentil stew, Esau sold his birthright, which we are told he despised, fulfilling what the Lord said to Rebekah about the older serving the younger (Genesis 25:30-34). From the time he came out of the womb holding his brother's heel, Jacob seemed determined to be first.

Like Ishmael and Isaac, we are given another example of human nature versus the spiritual nature. Esau, the firstborn, who should have been heir to the promise by tradition, was outwitted by his brother to give up that right, and he didn't even care. He wanted what he wanted right at the moment, not considering the consequences of his desire for immediate gratification. Jacob, waiting patiently and seizing the moment, by sheer determination got what he desperately wanted.

In today's society, instant gratification is the name of the game. We don't want to wait in line for anything, and we don't have to. One click of a mouse, and Amazon has your purchase at your door in a day or two. Talk to Alexa, and she can turn the stove on, change the temperature in the house, turn the lights on, and so much more. We don't even have to be home. Hard work is getting to be a thing of the past in some sectors of life.

We can garner a lot from what took place in the lives of these four people. We shouldn't just read about them. We should learn from them.

Lord, teach me to wait patiently for You when I am looking for answers. Help me especially in my family relations to look to You when difficulties arise that I see no answers for. There are many families in this world who are struggling, yet don't go to You in prayer. When the going gets tough they walk away from You. Help my family be the godly family You intend so that we honor You and are an example to those who are looking for answers from You. In Jesus' name, I pray. Amen.

Day 64

Isaac and Abimelek

Genesis 26:1-18

Isaac's life in chapter 26 is almost a mirror image of his father's. He left the land where he resided because of famine, and ended up in the land of the Philistines, a place called Gerar. Apparently, he intended to go to Egypt just as his father had, but "The Lord appeared to Isaac and said, 'Do not go down to Egypt; live in the land where I tell you to live'" (Genesis 26:2). So, Isaac stayed where he was. At that time, God told Isaac he would be heir to the same promises as his father Abraham, if he obeyed Him. He did obey, which is somewhat troubling when we come to this next event.

It seems the men in Gerar took a liking to Isaac's wife, and he became afraid. "He thought, 'The men of this place might kill me on account of Rebekah, because she is beautiful'" (Genesis 26:7). Like father like son, Isaac lied about Rebekah being his wife and said she was his sister. Unlike Sarah, she apparently wasn't taken into Abimelek's harem or given to someone to be their wife.

"When Isaac had been there a long time, Abimelek king of the Philistines looked down from a window and saw Isaac caressing his wife Rebekah. So Abimelek summoned Isaac and said, 'She is really your wife! Why did you say, "She is my sister"?'" When Isaac explained his dilemma, Abimelek gave him a harsh rebuke, but then ordered his people not to molest either Isaac or Rebekah, or they would be put to death (Genesis 26:8-11).

Isaac came clean when confronted with his lie. It must have broken any trust that existed between him and Abimelek, as it does for anyone who lies. It takes a long time to rebuild trust once broken. There are six things God hates, seven that are detestable to Him, and one of them is a lying tongue (Proverbs 6:16-19). Let's think twice, even three times, before ever lying!

Isaac remained in the land and prospered greatly, so much so that the Philistines envied him, which ultimately led Abimelek to tell Isaac to "move away from us; you have become too powerful for us" (Genesis 26:16). Isaac then moved to the Valley of Gerar where disputes also arose. He was a quiet man, and apparently wanted to avoid confrontation. He packed up and continued moving, digging and unplugging wells wherever he went, until he dug a third well which no one quarreled over, naming it "Rehoboth," saying, "Now the Lord has given us room and we will flourish in the land" (Genesis 26:22).

Tracing Isaac's journey, it seems all the disputes and quarreling actually led him to the place where the Lord wanted him to be, ending up in Beersheba, where God appeared to him. There, Isaac's life took a major turn. "That night the Lord appeared to him and said, 'I am the God of your father Abraham. Do not be afraid, for I am with you; I will bless you and will increase the number of your descendants for the sake of my servant Abraham.' Isaac built an altar there and called on the name of the Lord. There he pitched a tent, and there his servants dug a well" (Genesis 26:23-25).

Isaac finally found peace when he came to the place God wanted him to be. He put God first, which is a wonderful example for us to follow in our own walk with the Lord. When we seek first His kingdom, He provides for our needs (Matthew 6:33).

Lord, check me in my spirit if I am ever tempted to lie. May I always be truthful in my dealings with others, remembering to seek first Your kingdom above all else in order to remain faithful. In Jesus' name, I pray. Amen.

Day 65

A Sworn Agreement, Again

Genesis 26:19-34

When Abimelek showed up sometime later with his advisor and commander, Isaac wasn't too impressed with his arrival and asked him, "Why have you come to me, since you were hostile to me and sent me away?" (Genesis 26:27). I probably would have asked the same question if I'd been told to leave the place where I had become quite wealthy and prospered greatly, then had to pick up and leave because of envy and jealousy. Their answer was forthright: "We saw clearly that the Lord was with you; so we said, 'There ought to be a sworn agreement between us'" (Genesis 26:28). They were looking for a mutual agreement between them to not harm each other, and Isaac was okay with that.

This may be a good example of what Jesus told us to do when he said, "But I tell you, love your enemies and pray for those who persecute you, that you may be children of your Father in heaven" (Matthew 5:44-45). I wouldn't say Abimelek was necessarily an enemy, but he certainly wasn't an ally.

It's always best to pray for the Lord's guidance and direction when it comes to any decision we need to make. It may not be likely that we will ever be in a position to sign an agreement with someone who at one time was unfriendly to us, but there are many aspects of life to which this could apply. Keep in mind that when others see those who live a life for Christ, they see something different than what the world has to offer. Who knows? It may lead to their salvation one day.

Isaac prepared a feast, and early the next morning the men swore an oath to each other. Isaac sent them away, and they left in peace. That very day Isaac was blessed when his servants came and told him about a well that they dug saying, "We have found water!" (Genesis 26:32). It's in our obedience to Him that we are blessed.

Lord, thank You once again for the Scriptures. No matter what anyone says, this Book of books gives me guidance for how to live by learning from those who came before me. Though it is not a history book of the world, it is Your history of Your people. And though they were far from perfect, You are always perfect and faithful. May I learn from their mistakes and become a more faithful follower of Christ because of what You are teaching me. In Jesus' name, I pray. Amen.

Day 66

Blessing Through Deception

Genesis 27:1-40

Though they were twin brothers, Esau and Jacob could not have been more different from each other. Esau, the outdoors and woodsy guy, was on the hunt, always looking for excitement. Jacob stayed close to home, a mama's boy, learning how to cook and keep the home fires burning.

Isaac was old and blind when he called Esau to give him a blessing. He first asked his son, though, to prepare his favorite food. Why Isaac needed a meal before giving the blessing is uncertain, but it sure opened up a door of opportunity for his other son. Rebekah listened in on this conversation and had a plan. While Esau was hunting, she prepared tasty food for Jacob to give to his father. Then she told her son Jacob to take it to his father so he could receive the blessing.

Jacob feared his father would know it wasn't Esau, and instead of receiving a blessing he would be cursed for trying to trick his father. That didn't faze Rebekah one bit. She had a ready answer. "My son, let the curse fall on me. Just do what I say" (Genesis 27:13). Rebekah not only prepared the food, she took the best clothes of Esau and put them on Jacob. Then she covered his hands and the smooth part of his neck with the goatskins (Esau was a hairy man), and Jacob went to his father. It is as though she had been preparing all along for this very opportunity.

"Isaac asked his son, 'How did you find it so quickly, my son?' 'The Lord your God gave me success,' he replied. Then Isaac said to Jacob, 'Come near so I can touch you, my son, to know whether you really are my son Esau.' Jacob went close to his father Isaac, who touched him and said, 'The voice is the voice of Jacob, but the hands are the hands of Esau.' So he proceeded to bless him" (Genesis 27:20-23).

I've never understood why Rebekah did this. Before the twins were born, she prayed to God, and He told her the older would serve the younger. Since she knew this, why didn't she continue to pray and believe it would work out instead of deceiving her own husband, and then instructing her son to lie to his father? Then again, why did Isaac secretly call Esau to receive a blessing without letting Rebekah and Jacob know about it?

That's sometimes how families are, aren't they? How many secrets lie at the root of family chaos and bitterness? Or how many times have we gone ahead of the Lord because we didn't want to wait for Him to answer in His timing because we wanted a different outcome than what He planned? If we don't do things God's way, there is always strife, especially when lying is involved.

When Esau returned to his father, he was shocked to hear Isaac ask, "Who are you?"

"I am your son," he answered, "your firstborn, Esau."

"Isaac trembled violently" – he must have been so angry – "and said, 'Who was it, then, that hunted game and brought it to me? I ate it just before you came and I blessed him—and indeed he will be blessed!'"

Can you hear the gut-wrenching voice of Esau as he might have slid across the floor on his knees and with a loud, bitter cry said to his father, "Bless me – me too, my father!"

Isaac answered him, "Your brother came deceitfully and took your blessing" (Genesis 27:32-35).

Esau did not give up, but insisted, "Do you have only one blessing, my father? Bless me too, my father!"

"His father Isaac answered him, 'Your dwelling will be away from the earth's richness, away from the dew of heaven above. You will live by the sword and you will serve your brother. But when you grow restless, you will throw his yoke from off your neck'" (Genesis 27:38-40).

That sounds more like a curse than a blessing, but Esau insisted and that's what he received.

Here is a family of God torn apart because Isaac's wife, like Abraham's wife Sarah, didn't wait upon the Lord but came up with her own solution for what she perceived was a problem. What must the Lord have thought during all the drama that was taking place? Nothing is said about any of them praying at any time.

Waiting is not something we are very good at. "But those who hope in the Lord will renew their strength. They will soar on wings like eagles; they will run and not grow weary; they will walk and not be faint" (Isaiah 40:31). Those are blessings worth waiting for.

Lord, help me not look for the easy way around things, which often results in lying and deceit to get intended results. May I always call upon You for strength to be truthful in everything I think, do and say, so that You will be honored, and I will be at peace. In Jesus' name, I pray. Amen.

Day 67

Jacob Flees

Genesis 27:41 - 28:9

If Rebekah and Jacob knew the serious consequences of their deceit and trickery, maybe they would have thought more clearly about what they were doing. But like most sinful acts, we often do not think about that until it is too late.

Esau was so angry, the grudge he held against his brother began to boil like a hot caldron, and he said to himself, "The days of mourning for my father are near; then I will kill my brother Jacob" (Genesis 27:41).

Rebekah learned of this and instructed Jacob to flee at once to her brother Laban. Unfortunately for both of them, this became more than a short separation. It would be twenty years before Jacob returned, and it appears Rebekah never saw her son again; at least that we have knowledge of. How heartbreaking.

Before sending Jacob off, Rebekah complained bitterly to her husband about the Hittite women (referring to those Esau had married). She didn't want Jacob's wife to be a Hittite. She was so distressed, she said, "My life will not be worth living" (Genesis 27:46). It was a dramatic urging for Isaac to do something.

Isaac called for Jacob, possibly feeling he had no choice if he wanted to please his wife. He blessed Jacob again and sent him away with a commandment to take a wife from among the daughters of Laban, his mother's brother. He added to his blessing, saying, "May God Almighty bless you and make you fruitful and increase your numbers until you become a community of peoples. May he give you and your descendants the blessing given to Abraham, so that you may take possession of the land where you now reside as a foreigner, the land God gave to Abraham." Then Isaac sent Jacob on his way (Genesis 28:3-5).

When Esau learned of this additional blessing on Jacob by his father, he realized how displeasing the Canaanite (Hittite) women were to his father Isaac. So, he married one of Ishmael's daughters, in addition to the wives he already had. Sadly, it was too little too late to please his father by marrying one of Abraham's granddaughters; especially a daughter of Ishmael, the son born to Hagar, who was not the heir of Abraham's covenant with God.

When we try making things right by our own efforts, excluding any thought of God in our decisions, it still does not bring a blessing from Him, something which Esau apparently did not understand.

That is a lot to absorb, isn't it? It has all the elements of intrigue needed for a movie; but this is real life. It actually happened, and these are God's people! As Robert Deffinbaugh of the Community Bible Chapel in Richardson, Texas, said in a sermon on Esau and Jacob, "Man's sin can never frustrate the will of God but it can fulfill it." Then he added, "The sins of Isaac, Esau, Rebekah, and Jacob did not in any way thwart God's will from being done."[1]

His will was that the children of promise were to come through Jacob, not Esau. Rebekah knew this before her sons were born.

Lord, I don't want to live in a world of lies and deceit, but that is exactly where I am. Help me keep my thoughts fixed on Jesus so that I will remain faithful to You all the days of my life. In Jesus' name, I pray. Amen.

Day 68

Jacob's Dream

Genesis 28:10-22

Jacob quickly fled from everything he had ever known. Did he feel regret over deceiving his father and betraying his brother? Was he angry with his mother for devising such a plan that went awry? Was he feeling alone and forsaken, not knowing what to expect when he arrived at his uncle's home? It's not far-fetched to believe this was a very emotional time for him.

At some point in his journey, he got tired and stopped for the night as the sun set. He took a stone, put it under his head, and lay down to sleep. He had a dream; more like a revelation of God's plan. When he awoke, he knew he had had an encounter with God. I'd like to think it was an ah-ha moment for Jacob, when for the first time he heard directly from God.

When was your ah-ha moment when you realized you couldn't do life without Jesus? I remember mine. A friend invited me to the Assembly of God church she attended. For someone who was brought up in the Catholic faith, this was quite different, but I'm so glad I went! I can't remember anything about the sermon. What I do remember is at the end, the pastor asked those who wanted to be forgiven of their sins to come forward and ask Jesus into their heart, and I did. My life has never been the same.

Neither was Jacob's. We are never the same once we have been touched by God. "[Jacob] was afraid and said, 'How awesome is this place! This is none other than the house of God; this is the gate to heaven'" (Genesis 28:17). Then he set up a pillar and poured oil on top of it to mark the exact place. He called the place Bethel, meaning "the house of God,"[1] from its previous name of Luz, meaning "almond tree."[2]

Have you noticed a pattern? Every time someone has an encounter with God, there is a name change, such as Abram to Abraham, Sarai to Sarah, and now Luz to Bethel.

Once we experience God's presence, our lives don't magically become carefree and less burdensome. But there is a new hope, a new trust, a new relationship with our Savior that leads us into a better life in and through Him. Therefore, it should not be difficult, as Peter wrote to "rid yourselves of all malice and all deceit, hypocrisy, envy, and slander of every kind. Like newborn babies, crave pure spiritual milk, so that by it you may grow up in your salvation, now that you have tasted that the Lord is good" (1 Peter 2:1-3).

"Then Jacob made a vow, saying, 'If God will be with me and will watch over me on this journey I am taking and will give me food to eat and clothes to wear so that I return safely to my father's household, then the Lord will be my God" (Genesis 28:20-21).

That's what happens when Jesus enters our hearts; the Spirit of God becomes our guide, and we have a desire to please only Him, to pray and ask for His will and not our own. We also have the knowledge that He is always with us, and we can trust Him with our lives.

Lord, thank You again for giving me Your Word so that I can read about those who came before me. You saw them where they were, and You called them to You. May You do the same for me when I cry out to You. In Jesus' name, I pray. Amen.

Day 69

All in the Family

Genesis 29:1-14

There is no way I can know how Jacob was feeling as he continued his journey to Harran, but I would venture to say he might have been walking with his head held a little higher, maybe even with a bounce in his step. He also might have had no idea what he was facing when he arrived, but somehow it didn't matter. God was with him.

When Jacob got to the place where shepherds tended their flocks, "Jacob asked the shepherds, 'My brothers, where are you from?'

"'We're from Harran,' they replied.

"He said to them, 'Do you know Laban, Nahor's grandson?'

"'Yes, we know him,' they answered.

"Then Jacob asked them, 'Is he well?'

"'Yes, he is,' they said, 'and here comes his daughter Rachel with the sheep'" (Genesis 29:4-6).

Jacob ended up at a well as he was on his way to find a wife, just like Abraham's servant who went looking for a wife for Isaac. The first woman Jacob saw was Laban's daughter, whom he later married, but the way he gets there is nothing like the marriage of Isaac and Rebekah.

The shepherds whom Jacob met were waiting around the well until all shepherds arrived so they could roll the heavy stone away, water the flocks, then together replace the stone. But when Jacob saw Rachel, he went over and rolled the stone away from the mouth of the well so she could water her sheep. He was so excited to learn his uncle was well, he kissed Rachel and began to weep aloud. When he told Rachel who he was, she ran home to tell her father, Laban. He, too, was excited and hurried to meet Jacob, whom he embraced and brought to his home.

Jacob told Laban why he was there, though it's doubtful he explained the trickery he and his mother played on his father. "Then Laban said to him, 'You are my own flesh and blood'" (Genesis 29:14).

Jacob was greeted with open arms, and for the first time in a while, it sounds like one big happy family, right? Outward appearances are not always an indication of what is really going on. Trouble was stirring, but it would take years for Jacob to discover.

Many families, including Christians, struggle with family issues. We want others to think everything is wonderful, when often it is not. We don't have to shout our troubles from the rooftops, but we can be honest with our heavenly Father about them, and go to Him in prayer. We can approach His throne of grace with confidence, where we will find mercy and grace to help us in our time of need (Hebrews 4:16).

Lord, teach me to pray earnestly when I am in need. I don't want to pretend there are no problems just because I want others to think I have it all together. I struggle in my relationships, Lord, and I need help to figure it out. Thank You that You are with me, and that You do hear me when I pray. In Jesus' name, I pray. Amen.

Day 70

Jacob Deceived

Genesis 29:15-30

During my research for this Genesis devotional, I've found many reliable sources to help me with particularly difficult passages. There is often a majority of agreement on many portions of Scripture, but when it came to Laban, Jacob, Leah, and Rachel, opinions were all over the place. I've spent time in prayer asking for direction on what we can glean from what took place in Genesis 29:15-30, and this is what I'll share.

"After Jacob had stayed with him for a whole month, Laban said to him, 'Just because you are a relative of mine, should you work for me for nothing? Tell me what your wages should be'" (Genesis 29:14-15).

It sounds like Jacob had been giving Laban free labor, but this also gave Jacob a chance to get to know Rachel better. "Jacob was in love with Rachel and said, 'I'll work for you seven years in return for your younger daughter Rachel'" (Genesis 29:18).

This is in stark contrast to Isaac and Rebekah. When Abraham sent his servant to find a wife for Isaac, he came prepared with many gifts and supplies to give to Rebekah's family. After Rebekah agreed to go, she and Isaac were married immediately. Jacob, on the other hand, left home quickly. Though his father had blessed him, it doesn't appear he gave Jacob financial or emotional support for choosing a wife. The only thing Jacob could offer was his labor in return for a wife.

A big celebration followed those seven years. Jacob was prepared to receive his wife. Unbeknownst to him, Laban gave Jacob his oldest daughter, Leah, instead of Rachel, which Jacob discovered the next morning.

Scripture says, "Leah had weak eyes" (Genesis 29:17). The Hebrew word for "weak" here actually means "tender" or "delicate."[1] Perhaps she was more of the quiet type, less assertive than her younger sister, but not necessarily homely or difficult to look upon. But that did nothing to console Jacob.

Although distressed when he discovered Laban's deceit, it was too late. The marriage with Leah had been consummated, and she was now Jacob's wife. But Jacob loved Rachel and wanted her as his wife. So, after a week with Leah, Laban gave Rachel to Jacob. Jacob then worked an additional seven years for Laban.

Consequences always follow our actions, either good or bad. Had Rebekah and Jacob not conspired to trick Isaac, God would have made the way for Jacob to receive the blessing of the firstborn. Instead of having to run away, Jacob may have had his father's blessing in choosing a wife, as well as financial stability to take care of her without having to work for someone else. If so, he would not have been deceived by his father-in-law to take both daughters in marriage.

These are all "what ifs," so we will never know what God's original plan was. What we do know is that God did not take His blessing from Jacob. And though Jacob loved Rachel more than Leah, it was Leah through whom Jesus, the Savior, came to earth; not Rachel.

This story would have been different had there been honesty. Even though I've written about this subject a lot, I believe it cannot be emphasized enough that lying is wrong. So, when we find ourselves thinking there's a better way than God's way, we should take a step back and consider the consequences of lying or deceiving someone to get what we want. It just isn't worth the turmoil that follows. God's way is always best.

Lord, help me to always be honest with You, with myself, and with others. When there are times I am doubtful about which way to turn, may I always turn to You for guidance so that the choice I make honors You. In Jesus' name, I pray. Amen.

Day 71

Jacob's Children

Genesis 29:31-30:24

One person often overlooked in this story is Leah. Imagine knowing that when they awoke in the morning, Jacob would discover it wasn't Rachel, and Leah would be spurned by her husband. She had fortitude, though, and didn't wallow in her sorrow. She took full advantage of being Jacob's first wife.

After the birth of their first son, she said, "It is because the Lord has seen my misery. Surely my husband will love me now" (Genesis 29:32). She had a longing, a desire, to be loved by her husband. Wouldn't you? It's not often a woman has to contend with her sister for the love of her husband, but that was the situation.

Leah conceived again, ultimately giving birth to four sons. What a disappointment that the birth of these sons did not bring her husband to her side. She overcame that disappointment, though, by giving praise to the Lord (Genesis 29:35).

"When Rachel saw that she was not bearing Jacob any children, she became jealous of her sister. So she said to Jacob, 'Give me children, or I'll die!' Jacob became angry with her and said, 'Am I in the place of God, who has kept you from having children?'" (Genesis 30:1-2).

History repeats itself in that like Sarah, Rachel, who was unable to have children, gave her concubine to Jacob in order to have children, and she had two. When Leah realized she couldn't have any more children, she gave Jacob her concubine, and she had two children. Later, the two sisters resolved an argument by bargaining for time with Jacob, which is what Leah wanted.

Up to this point, Leah is the only one praying to God. He heard her plea and saw her misery. She conceived yet a fifth son, then a sixth. Then Leah said, "God has presented me with a precious gift. This time my husband will treat me with honor, because I have borne him six sons" (Genesis 30:20). Sometime later she and Jacob had a daughter named Dinah.

Rachel's attitude changed, and she began praying to God. God remembered Rachel, and opened her womb. When her son Joseph was born, she said, "God has taken away my disgrace. . .May the Lord add to me another son," (Genesis 30:23-24), which eventually He did.

The person we can learn from the most in this story is Leah. She had a constant rivalry with her sister because Jacob loved Rachel. Leah longed to be loved by her husband as well. She was disappointed that he did not love her, even after bearing him six sons, but she overcame her disappointment through prayer and praise.

How will we react when the one we love doesn't love us back? Will we remain disappointed and have a pity party, or will we seek God and praise Him? God will never disappoint us. He always loves us, for God is love, and whoever lives in love lives in God, and God in him (1 John 4:16).

Lord, there are times I will disappoint others and they will disappoint me, but no matter what, may I always look to You for my source of true love and comfort. In Jesus' name, I pray. Amen.

Day 72

Jacob's Flocks Increase

Genesis 30:25 - 31:1-2

Fourteen years passed since Jacob arrived in Harran. He'd been a hard worker, but it appears his wages were not enough to provide for his large family. Jacob wanted to go back to his homeland, but Laban wasn't quite ready for that. He said, "I have learned by divination that the Lord has blessed me because of you. Name your wages, and I will pay them" (Genesis 30:27-28).

By this time, Jacob must have known Laban had an ulterior motive and had perhaps given some thought as to what he would do if Laban insisted he stay. He responded to Laban, "Don't give me anything. But if you will do this one thing for me, I will go on tending your flocks and watching over them" (Genesis 30:31).

Once Jacob revealed his plan to remove all the speckled sheep and goats, as well as dark-colored lambs, Laban agreed. Jacob knew the flocks and their habits quite well. He'd been taking care of them for fourteen years, and possibly tended sheep for his father before that. He had a plan. After implementing his plan, Jacob grew exceedingly prosperous and came to own large flocks, maidservants, menservants, camels and donkeys. Laban was upset about this change of events, and he changed his attitude toward Jacob.

Life often gives us lemons when we're looking for sweet, ripened oranges. Maybe we've been in a job where our boss has taken advantage of us, or a co-worker asked for help on a project and then took full credit . Like Jacob, we might feel unappreciated and taken advantage of; but also like Jacob, we needn't become bitter.

A job change may not be possible, but a change of our hearts is. Scripture tells us, "Whatever you do, work at it with all your heart, as working for the Lord, not for human masters, since you know that you will receive an inheritance from the Lord as your reward" (Colossians 3:23-24). Jacob did just that, and God blessed him.

This doesn't mean we will be prosperous in this world, but there's no question we will be with Jesus in the next (Luke 23:43). If we have been wronged, God remains faithful. He sees everything that everyone does, and "Anyone who does wrong will be repaid for their wrongs, and there is no favoritism" (Colossians 3:25).

Lord, Your story is so awesome. Thank You for including the life stories of men and women who, like us, have had trials and hardships. Thank You also that we are made perfect in You. I know I am a work in progress, Lord. Like the potter, make and mold me until I am conformed to the image and likeness of Your Son, our Savior. In Jesus' name, I pray. Amen.

Day 73

Reconciliation

Genesis 31:1-18

Jacob had no doubt about going back to his own country after the Lord said to him, "Go back to the land of your fathers and to your relatives, and I will be with you" (Genesis 31:3). I would have done most anything to have heard a message like that from God; maybe I wouldn't have stayed away from my own family as long as I did. But there's no going back, and I know that.

If we have continual regrets about our decisions, we get stuck like a car in a ditch. It's nearly impossible for God to use us until we deal with what's preventing us from moving forward. I believe He shows us the things in our lives that get us stuck. When He does, it's up to us to do something about it, and Jacob did.

He knew he'd fallen out of favor with Laban so he sent word to his wives to come to the field where the flocks were and he instructed them to get ready to leave. As Jacob explained the situation to his wives, we learn more about Laban and Jacob's relationship. We also learn it was God who provided the speckled, spotted, and streaked animals to take away Laban's livestock and give them to Jacob. God earlier showed Jacob in a dream that this is what He would do.

Jacob's wives seemed fed up with their father, and were ready to take advantage of their husband's good fortune. This time, Jacob didn't ask Laban; he just packed up all he owned and began the journey back to the land of Canaan. Was he afraid? Was he excited? What emotions might he have been feeling after all this time?

Reconciliation is difficult, especially when you've been gone as long as Jacob was. I know. I was separated from my family for over thirty years before seeking reconciliation, and we're still trying to figure it out. But it is not difficult with God, for "if anyone is in Christ, the new creation has come. The old has gone, the new is here! All this is from God, who reconciled us to himself through Christ and gave us the ministry of reconciliation: that God was reconciling the world to himself in Christ, not counting people's sins against them" (2 Corinthians 5:17-19).

Isn't that amazing? Once we were separated from God because of our sins but now—thank You, Jesus—we are reconciled, and on our way home to heaven because of what Christ did for us on the cross. What greater gift could God have given us than that!

Lord, thank You for the gift of reconciliation. I rejoice in what You have done for me, so thankful that I no longer have to live in my sinful ways, far away from You and lost in this world without hope. Teach me each day how to be better equipped to share the good news of Jesus Christ with others so they too may have reconciliation with You. In Jesus' name, I pray. Amen.

Day 74

Rachel Takes Laban's Household Gods

Genesis 31:19

I've often thought of the people in the Old Testament in terms of those who followed God and those who didn't. When it came to those who were unfaithful, I sort of skipped over them. I realize now I've missed a lot with that attitude. These are people with thoughts, emotions, and reasons for doing things, just like us, and we can learn from them, too.

Such is the case with Rachel. I've always been puzzled as to why she stole her father's household gods. Whatever her reasons, I think it's safe to assume she was self-centered. She felt confident in her relationship with Jacob because she knew he loved her more than her older sister. She took advantage by antagonizing Leah, and she also deceived her father. She had to have known taking her father's gods would upset him, but she did it anyway.

These household gods were small statues, not necessarily worshiped by those who kept them, but possibly representing deceased family members.[1] They also could have served as titles of ownership to one's property and inheritance.[2]

Rachel may have taken them because she knew she would never return home to see her father or relatives, and she wanted something important to remember them by. Or perhaps she just didn't want her father to have them. I lean more toward the former because she chose to take them with her rather than destroy or bury them. Either way, they were not hers to take. Had she been discovered, serious consequences could have included death.

We never learn why Rachel took these household gods, and it appears her deceit was never discovered. But God knew, and that is what should be our guide if we ever consider lying to or deceiving someone (Numbers 32:23b). The truth is what sets us free (John 8:32).

Lord, thank You for Your goodness and mercy toward me, even when I am not always honest and, at times, am downright deceitful. I've even tested You – oh, how arrogant! – by praying about something I knew was wrong but wanted You to condone it. Forgive me, Father, for ever having such a deceitful attitude. Search me, cleanse me, and continually change me so that I may be the child of God You desire me to be. In Jesus' name, I pray. Amen.

Day 75

A Covenant Between Adversaries

Genesis 31:20-55

By the time Laban caught up to Jacob's caravan, he was steaming mad. He knew better than to say anything good or bad to Jacob, though, because God admonished him in a dream. Though he didn't harm Jacob, Laban let him know the only reason he wasn't taking retribution was because God warned him not to.

One matter was heavy on Laban's mind. We can imagine his indignant tone toward Jacob when he asked, "But why did you steal my gods?" Now it was Jacob's turn to be incensed. He had no idea what Laban was talking about, and challenged him to search his entire camp to find what Laban was looking for, adding, "If you find anyone who has your gods, that person shall not live" (Genesis 31:32).

Laban made an extensive search of all the tents, but when he came to Rachel's tent she was sitting on the very place she hid the household gods. She said to her father, "Don't be angry, my lord, that I cannot stand up in your presence; I'm having my period" (Genesis 31:35). She knew exactly how to continue her deceit because in those days when women were having their period it was connected to impurity. Since impurity was contagious, the women were isolated and untouchable.

Laban searched but did not find the household gods, which made Jacob even more infuriated. He let loose on Laban like a burst dam, the water pouring out with enough force to destroy everything in its path. Laban then took a different approach to calm the waters by offering a solution to their problem, "Come now, let's make a covenant, you and I, and let it serve as a witness between us" (Genesis 31:44).

When tempers are high, situations can quickly escalate to a fever pitch. Jacob felt justified in leaving without telling Laban; Laban felt betrayed, and Rachel seemingly got away with her deception. God spoke to both of these men and, when they finished venting, they began to think rationally about a solution to their problem.

Ephesians 4:25-27 says, "Therefore each of you must put off falsehood and speak truthfully to your neighbor, for we are all members of one body. In your anger do not sin. Do not let the sun go down while you are still angry, and do not give the devil a foothold."

Jacob and Laban were able to work through their difficulties, even having a meal together. Early the next morning, Laban kissed his grandchildren and daughters, and blessed them. Then he returned home.

Anger, bitterness, resentment, and self-justification result in even more anger, bitterness, resentment, and self-justification. As Christ-followers, we are told to "do nothing out of selfish ambition or vain conceit. Rather, in humility value others above yourselves" (Philippians 2:3). Then we can listen to what others are saying, and ask the Lord in prayer for a resolution. In this way, all concerned can go away with a sense of peace, resulting in a blessing.

Lord, when I find myself in a heated argument trying to make my point without listening to what the other person is saying, check me and help me stop immediately. I know I am guilty of doing this very thing. I pray that when this happens, I will be sensitive to the Holy Spirit's prompting to listen, pray, and seek Your help in finding a resolution that will bring peace and blessing to all involved. In Jesus' name, I pray. Amen.

Day 76

The Unknown

Genesis 32:1-2

Jacob's past was behind him, but now he faced an uncertain future. How could he continue on this journey into the unknown? He couldn't open his Bible and read Psalm 34:17 which says, "The righteous cry out and the Lord hears them; he delivers them from all their troubles," or

1 Peter 5:7, "Cast all your anxiety on him [Jesus] because he cares for you." No, he didn't have God's Word to comfort and guide him, like we do, but he had faith, and as he went on his way, "the angels of God met him. When Jacob saw them, he said, 'This is the camp of God!'" (Genesis 32:1-2).

The Lord did something extraordinary in Jacob's life, and Jacob took time to think about it. He memorialized this experience by naming the place Mahanaim, meaning "two camps."[1] It was the place where Jacob's past and future met.

Jacob had changed considerably since leaving his family. He was no longer Rebekah's favorite son who deceived and connived to get what he wanted. Now he was confident, for he knew God was with him.

Jacob's excitement must have welled up within him, like a volcano ready to burst. He was ready to walk into the unknown with his family, and possessions, toward the place God called him.

May we be like Jacob and look to the Lord to help us forget what is behind and strain toward what is ahead. May we press on toward the goal to win the prize for which God has called us heavenward in Christ Jesus (Philippians 3:13-14). Let's have confidence to trust God with our past and move forward toward our future, even when it is unknown.

Lord, with gratitude I receive the victories You have given me. Help me see where I have been and how You have brought me through, so I may go on my way knowing whatever lies ahead, You are with me. In Jesus' name, I pray. Amen.

Day 77

Jacob Prepares to Meet Esau

Genesis 32:3-21

It was difficult for Jacob to return to the family he had separated from for so long. I should know. I've written about how I was separated from my family for over thirty years. The thought of reaching out for possible reconciliation was overwhelming. I wasn't sure where to begin, so I began by praying for God's help and guidance. Then, I proceeded step by step, which did result in reconciliation.

Even after his encounter with God, Jacob had misgivings as he gathered his family and belongings to continue this journey. Twenty years passed since he fled for his life to find safety among his mother's relatives. Now God told him to return to the land that was promised to Abraham and Isaac, and there was no turning back.

Jacob's brother, Esau, lived in that land, and there had been no contact between them during Jacob's absence. Jacob didn't know if his parents were alive. He didn't know if Esau still harbored thoughts of murder against him for stealing the birthright, as well as receiving the blessing from their father. In his uncertainty, he formed a plan. It began by sending messengers ahead to find Esau and tell him, "Your servant Jacob says, 'I have been staying with Laban and have remained there till now'" (Genesis 32:4).

After the messengers returned and told Jacob Esau was coming to meet him with four hundred men, that surely wasn't the response Jacob was hoping for. He became more fearful and distressed.

Times of fear are opportunities for prayer. Whatever frightens us should drive us to our knees and to our God,[1] and it did for Jacob.

Jacob divided the people and then prayed. He sent five separate herds of animals to meet Esau, and instructed his servants to say to Esau each time, "Jacob is coming behind us." Then Jacob was alone and had another encounter with God (Genesis 32:18-19).

It takes faith and courage to trust God when we're faced with daunting circumstances and decisions. James knew this when he wrote to the twelve tribes of Israel scattered among the nations, "Consider it pure joy, my brothers and sisters, whenever you face trials of many kinds, because you know that the testing of your faith produces perseverance. Blessed is the one who perseveres under trial because, having stood the test, that person will receive the crown of life that the Lord has promised to those who love him" (James 1:2-3, 12).

Lord, what hope I have in You when I trust You with my struggles. May I never forget You are my mighty tower, the one I can turn to in times of uncertainty and struggles. In Jesus' name, I pray. Amen.

Day 78

Jacob Overcomes and is Blessed

Genesis 32:22-32

This may have been the first time in a long time Jacob was alone with no distractions to steer him away from what God had for him. That night, after sending his wives, concubines, and eleven sons over the ford of the Jabbok River, he met a man (or so he thought at first), and wrestled with him until daybreak. Jacob was so intent on winning this struggle, he would not let go.

Have you ever struggled with God, praying so intently that unless you received an answer you would not let go? There have not been many of those times in my life, but there is one I vividly remember.

My attempt to mend relationships with my family has been an emotional roller coaster that has not yet stopped to let its passengers disembark. While my dad was alive, I frequently flew from Florida, where I lived at the time, to visit my family who lived in California. After my dad died, I continued to visit and stayed at my mom's house. On one such visit, I went out for a walk by myself. Upon my return to the house, I announced, "I'm back." I received no response, but I heard voices coming from upstairs. I didn't mean to eavesdrop, but I heard my name mentioned, and my ears perked up. What I overheard troubled me deeply. I walked out of the house feeling extremely hurt. In my distress, I was even ready to consider walking away again.

Instead, I went to a nearby park. I sat on a bench and prayed, determined not to leave until I received a word from the Lord. In my spirit, I heard Him say, "You are looking for affirmation in the wrong places. Look to Me."

The relief I felt is difficult to describe in words. I had been trying to please everyone in the family, get their approval, and force them to love me despite our differences. I took my focus off the Lord, and put it on them. The struggle was over, and I was at peace.

I'm not certain this was the type of struggle Jacob was having, but does it really matter? He was determined to get relief from God, and would not let go until he did. "When the man saw that he could not overpower him, he touched the socket of Jacob's hip so that his hip was wrenched as he wrestled with the man. Then the man said, 'Let me go, for it is daybreak.'

"But Jacob replied, 'I will not let go unless you bless me.'

"The man asked him, 'What is your name?'

"'Jacob,' he answered.

"Then the man said, 'Your name will no longer be Jacob, but Israel, because you have struggled with God and with humans and have overcome'" (Genesis 32:25-28).

This was such a transformational event that Jacob's name was changed to "Israel." He no longer was the man he used to be; He was a new person with a new name. Jacob was certainly rewarded for his tenaciousness.

"So Jacob called the place Peniel, saying, 'It is because I saw God face to face, and yet my life was spared'" (Genesis 32:30). Jacob was touched by God, and he was never the same.

When we give up our struggles with this world, and discover Jesus as Savior, we become a new creation in Him (2 Corinthians 5:17), and we are never the same.

Lord, may I come to the place where my struggles become blessings. In the process, help me let go of the old, and embrace the new. I give my heart, mind, soul, and spirit to You to conform to the image of Jesus Christ, my Savior and King. In Jesus' name, I pray. Amen.

Day 79

Jacob and Esau Meet

Genesis 33:1-20

The lives of Esau and Jacob have all the makings for an intriguing movie: hatred, thoughts of murder, fleeing to another land, lying, deceit, polygamy, sibling rivalry. What were these twin brothers expecting as they traveled towards each other? Esau was coming with four hundred men, and along the way encountered Jacob's servants who offered him gifts. Was Esau preparing for battle, yet beginning to soften each time he heard Jacob's servants say to him, "...Jacob is coming behind us"? Was Jacob, who just encountered God, wavering in his trust and worrying about Esau's intent toward him?

These are unanswered questions. One thing was certain: They were about to meet.

Fearful of what Esau might do, Jacob divided his family into four segments, and then he went ahead, bowing to the ground seven times as he approached his brother.

What was Esau's reaction? He threw his arms around Jacob's neck, and kissed him. Jacob's fears were finally put to rest.

There have been times I've tried to manipulate others so I could attain a certain outcome. I came to realize how wrong that was. God is not a conniver or a deceiver. He doesn't do things underhandedly. He is holy, always forthright, and honest in His actions. That is what He wants us to be (1 Peter 1:13-16).

Before her sons were born, God told Rebekah the older would serve the younger (Genesis 25:23). She hurt her sons and her husband when she came up with a scheme to get the result she wanted. How different it may have been if she trusted

God to work things out. But she didn't, and so we have this sad story of family disunity and distrust. Fortunately, Esau and Jacob made amends and reconciled.

Is there someone in your life you are separated from because of harsh words, deceit, or lying? If so, please pray right now, and consider reaching out to them. Just like Jacob, the response may surprise you.

Lord, when faced with situations that seem insurmountable, draw me to You by Your Holy Spirit so I will stop to pray, and seek Your guidance. I ask for patience to then wait upon You for an answer. In Jesus' name, I pray. Amen.

Day 80

Jacob's Sons Take Revenge

Genesis 34:1-31

After purchasing a plot of ground for one hundred pieces of silver from the sons of Hamor, the father of Shechem, Jacob pitched his tent. Then he set up an altar, and called it El Elohe Israel, meaning "the God of Israel"[1]

Jacob's daughter, Dinah, visited the women of the land and met a man named Shechem who violated her. When Dinah's brothers found out, they were furious.

Shechem fell in love with Dinah and wanted to marry her. Dinah's brothers agreed, on one condition: that all the men of their town be circumcised.

Those words may have sounded sweeter than honey, but in their hearts and minds, Dinah's brothers were devising a deceitful plan of retribution.

Shechem and his father agreed. They "went to the gate of their city to speak to the men of their city. 'These men are friendly toward us,' they said. 'Let them live in our land and trade in it; the land has plenty of room for them. We can marry their daughters and they can marry ours. Won't their livestock, their property and all their other animals become ours? So let us agree to their terms, and they will settle among us'" (Genesis 34:20-21, and 23).

Though these things hadn't been agreed to by Dinah's brothers, it sounds as though the other men in the city needed convincing so they would agree to the terms; and they did.

Dennis Prager, founder of the online non-profit Prager University, sums up the situation this way: "Jacob's sons were deceiving Hamor and Shechem, and Hamor and Shechem in turn were deceiving their clan. Genesis is filled with people deceiving other people—because Genesis describes the human condition. Only by acknowledging how bad the human condition is does one appreciate how necessary the rest of the Torah[2] is. It provides the moral guidelines to solve the problems of the human condition."[3]

While the men were still recovering and in pain, Simeon and Levi, Dinah's brothers, took their swords and attacked the unsuspecting city. They killed every male and then took their sister Dinah from Shechem's house. Their other brothers joined them and looted the city. They seized not only the flocks, herds, and donkeys, they also took the women and children. This included all the wealth and everything in the houses.

When Jacob discovered what they had done, he was furious. Before his death, Jacob said this about his sons, Simeon and Levi: "Their swords are weapons of violence. Let me not enter their council, let me not join their assembly, for they have killed men in their anger and hamstrung oxen as they pleased. Cursed be their anger, so fierce, and their fury, so cruel! I will scatter them in Jacob and disperse them in Israel" (Genesis 49:5-7).

I like to think people are telling the truth when I deal with them, especially in business. But that is not always the case, is it? I have a friend whose husband trusted his business partner, only to discover he was lying and stole all the assets of their company. He left my friend and her husband bankrupt. They wanted to take him to court and make him pay for what he'd done, but they didn't. They trusted the Lord to make things right. It didn't happen overnight, but their prayers were answered.

We are told in Scripture not to take revenge in our own way, even when we are deeply hurt or injured by someone else. God sees and knows everything, and we can trust Him to do the right thing (Colossians 3:25 and Hebrews 10:30-31).

Lord, thank You for not sugarcoating the actions of Your people in the Old Testament. What Jacob's sons did was deceitful and wrong, but let me not be their judge for I know I too have been deceitful and wrong. I don't know what Your judgment was on them, but I can be certain You did what was right and just. Help me always be truthful and do the right thing. When I have done wrong, help me acknowledge it quickly, ask forgiveness, and do all I can to make things right. In Jesus' name, I pray. Amen.

Day 81

New Beginnings

Genesis 35:1-15

We know from earlier references that Abraham had his servant swear he would not "get a wife for my son from the daughters of the Canaanites, among whom I am living" (Genesis 24:3). We also learned the Hittite women Esau married were a source of grief to Isaac and Rebekah (Genesis 26:34-35), And we learned Rachel stole her father's household gods (Genesis 31:19).

The peoples of the earth worshiped many gods. But there is only one, true God, and He chose Abraham, Isaac, and Jacob to follow Him. They may have been influenced to worship other gods while living among pagan people, but that was no longer to be tolerated. God told Jacob to "get rid of the foreign gods you have with you, and purify yourselves and change your clothes" (Genesis 35:2). Jacob heard from God, and said, "I will build an altar to God, who answered me in the day of my distress and who has been with me wherever I have gone" (Genesis 35:3).

When a life-changing event took place in the lives of God's chosen people, He did extraordinary things, including giving new names to those involved. "God said to [Jacob], 'Your name is Jacob, but you will no longer be called Jacob; your name will be Israel.' So he named him Israel. And God said to him, 'I am God Almighty; be fruitful and increase in number. A nation and a community of nations will come from you, and kings will be among your descendants. The land I gave to Abraham and Isaac I also give to you, and I will give this land to your descendants after you'" (Genesis 35:10-12).

It was a new beginning for Jacob, and he wanted it to be remembered for generations. So he set up a stone pillar at the place where God talked with him (Genesis 35:14).

We, too, have a new beginning when we accept Christ into our life. We become God's children, and part of His family.

"Now if we are children then we are heirs—heirs of God and co-heirs with Christ, if indeed we share in his sufferings in order that we may also share in His glory" (Romans 8:17).

When we believe in Jesus Christ as Savior, we become children of God, brothers and sisters of Christ, and we are gifted with the inheritance which belongs to Him who not only died on the cross for our sins, but was resurrected from the dead, and now sits at the right hand of God (Colossians 3:1).

Lord, thank You for new beginnings. It began with Abraham, who You called Your friend. May I, too, come into an intimate relationship with You, the one, true God, so I am known not only as Your child, but Your friend. In Jesus' name, I pray. Amen.

Day 82

The Deaths of Rachel and Isaac

Genesis 35:16-29

If Jacob thought life was going to be simpler after he returned wholeheartedly to God, he was about to discover it would be anything but. Soon thereafter, Rachel died while giving birth to their second son, Benjamin.

Reuben was Jacob's firstborn, the son of Leah. Immediately after Rachel's death, Reuben had sex with Bilhah, Jacob's concubine and Rachel's servant. This was like claiming your inheritance before the death of your father. It was much more than a sexual act, though. It was taking a position of leadership and authority.

Time and again, we read in Scripture about God's people doing unimaginable things not only against Him, but against others. If there were no consequences for our actions, our world would be in disarray. Nor would there be a reason for Jesus' death on the cross.

One of my favorite Scriptures is from Hebrews 4:13: "Nothing in all creation is hidden from God's sight. Everything is uncovered and laid bare before the eyes of him to whom we must give account." This should bring solace to our hearts, knowing there are consequences, and God is the ultimate and just judge.

Reuben not only disgraced himself, he lost the coveted privileges as Jacob's firstborn son. When Jacob was dying, he remembered what Reuben did, and he said, "Reuben, you are my firstborn, my might, the first sign of my strength, excelling in honor, excelling in power. Turbulent as the waters, you will no longer excel, for you went up onto your father's bed, onto my couch and defiled it" (Genesis 49:3-4).

Customs were different during those times, but the turmoil, struggle, and pain are the same today even if the circumstances are different. Just because Jacob's life changed, and he was fully committed to God, it didn't mean everything was going to be easy.

When I first became a Christian, I wondered if life would be boring, even uneventful. I thought I could just sit back, read the Bible, talk to God, and wait for Jesus to come back. I was not prepared for my rude awakening.

Christians can't expect life to be free from heartache (Luke 9:23; 2 Timothy 3:12). When we read about the lives of the prophets, judges, kings, and others in the Old Testament, their lives were extremely difficult. The same is true for those in the New Testament. The only apostle who is believed to have died a natural death was John. The rest were said to have been martyred.[1]

At the end of this chapter, Isaac died at 180 years old and was buried by his sons Esau and Jacob. Apparently, Isaac lived much longer than he thought he would. Not only were Esau and Jacob reconciled, most likely Jacob and Isaac were as well.

The twelve sons of Jacob are listed in a genealogy before the account of Isaac's death. This is significant in that it tells us Jacob (renamed Israel) is now the patriarch of the covenant made with Abraham and Isaac, and it is through him and the lineage of one of his sons that the Messiah will one day come.

Lord, sometimes life with Jesus seems harder than life without Him when I don't understand the pain and suffering I am experiencing. Help me, as Your child, to know that this world is full of pain and suffering, and it will always be this way until the end of time. May I receive Your grace and mercy during my trying times, and realize my life is meant to give glory and honor to You, even when I suffer. Until the day You take me home, or until Jesus returns, may I never forget You are with me all the days of my life. In Jesus' name, I pray. Amen.

Day 83

Esau's Descendants

Genesis 36

Sometimes I come to a chapter or verse in the Bible and wonder, "Why is this included? Is it really necessary to know this?" That was my question for Chapter 36, which includes a long list of previously unknown people, except for Esau, who God told his mother Rebekah would become one of two nations.

Why do we need to read about his descendants, most of whose names we cannot pronounce and probably won't remember by the time we finish reading them? The Bible was not only written to read and study, it gives us insight into the lives of real people who tell God's story.

You might ask, "What does that mean?" If you haven't noticed, there is a consistent theme taking place between those who serve God and those who do not, such as Cain and Abel; Ishmael and Isaac; Esau and Jacob.

Esau was a man of the world. Despite his careless behavior in forfeiting his birthright for a cup of stew and losing his father's blessing, he prospered. One thing was lacking. He did not serve the one, true God or even acknowledge His existence.

As God's story continues throughout the Old Testament, we will encounter Esau's descendants, who became known as Edomites. In the book of Exodus, when the Israelites requested permission to pass through their land, the Edomites refused. From that time, they were hostile toward Israel, the descendants of Abraham, Isaac, and Jacob (Numbers 20:14-21).

A website called Compelling Truth puts it this way, "Between the Old and New Testament times, the Edomites were once again controlled by the Jews and forced to embrace Judaism. In the Greek language that gained prominence during this time, their name became the Idumaeans. King Herod was an Idumaean and ruled at the time of the birth of Jesus; he also commanded the deaths of all males two years old and under in Bethlehem to kill the threat of a Jewish king (Matthew 2:16-18).

"The Edomites, by then known as the Idumaeans, eventually disappear from history. One of the last mentions of the Idumeans was a reference to the land of Idumea by the church leader Jerome around AD 400. The prediction that Esau (the Edomites) would serve Jacob (the Israelites) proved true."[1]

This is one more example of God's word coming to pass, helping to build the foundation upon which our faith is based.

Lord, keep me focused on Your purpose for everything written in Your Word. I may not remember it all or even understand everything, but thank You I can count on its truth. In Jesus' name, I pray. Amen.

Day 84

Jacob's Son Joseph

Genesis 37:1-11

The most prominent figure throughout the rest of Genesis is Jacob's eleventh son, Joseph, known as "the dreamer" by his brothers. Joseph was the son of Rachel, whom Jacob loved, and was highly favored. The result was jealousy among his older brothers.

When Joseph was seventeen, he had dreams. His father and brothers rebuked him when Joseph shared those dreams. They couldn't fathom that one day they would bow down to their younger brother. Little did they know, that is exactly what would happen.

I've learned from this story to trust the Lord in all circumstances of my life. When everything is going in the wrong direction, life seems hopeless and lonely, I don't lose faith in the Lord, because I believe He is faithful (Deuteronomy 7:9 and Hebrews 10:23).

When we are tried and tested, our response makes a difference in the final outcome. It's encouraging to know that with God's strength and help, like Joseph, we too can fulfill God's plan for our lives.

Thank You, Father, for Your faithfulness. I ask today to receive a measure of faith from You, and that this faith would continue to grow within me as I read Your Word and pray. Give me strength and hope to endure the trials of life, knowing Your faithfulness will bring me through. In Jesus' name, I pray. Amen.

Day 85

Sold into Slavery

Genesis 37:12-36

Joseph's ten older brothers were grazing their flocks in the fields when Jacob sent Joseph to see if all was well. When Joseph's brothers saw him at a distance, they conspired to kill him. They threw him into a cistern and took off the richly ornamented robe his father made him. Later, Reuben went to retrieve Joseph from the cistern, but he wasn't there. He had been sold by his other brothers to a passing caravan traveling to Egypt and then sold to Potiphar, one of Pharaoh's officials.

Joseph's brothers "slaughtered a goat and dipped the robe in the blood. They took the ornate robe back to their father and said, 'We found this. Examine it to see whether it is your son's robe.' He recognized it and said, 'It is my son's robe! Some ferocious animal has devoured him. Joseph has surely been torn to pieces'" (Genesis 37:31-33). Jacob was left to believe Joseph was eaten by a wild animal, and his other sons didn't tell him otherwise.

There is a lot going on in this family of God. Which family member can you relate to? Are you a jealous one? Maybe you're the favorite. Maybe you are an only child who thinks the world is yours because you are constantly the center of attention. Maybe that singleness causes resentment against your parents for not having more children. Or are you a parent who has lost a child?

No matter our situation, we all have feelings about who we are in our family and what we consider our rightful place to be. Most of us are never really satisfied, are we?

True satisfaction comes when we turn our eyes to the One who chose when, and to whom we were born. I believe Joseph knew this, and it gave him confidence—perhaps too much at times—to know that regardless of his circumstances, God was with him.

God is looking for those who will trust Him no matter their position in the family, their position at work, or their financial situation. He wants to know, "Will you trust Me every day no matter your circumstances?"

Joseph, like many of us, had more than his fair share of troubles. He was unwillingly taken from his family and sold into slavery. He was falsely accused of wrongdoing. He was forgotten, and forsaken in a dingy prison. He never once blamed God. He never wavered in his faith. As Christians, we should ask our Lord to help us be like Joseph so we will trust Him to bring us through life's disappointments and trials.

Lord, may my heart be filled with the knowledge that You are faithful, You are loving, You are kind, and You never forsake Your children in their time of need. Help me trust You more each day so that when difficulties come, I look to You for my source of strength. In Jesus' name, I pray. Amen.

Day 86

Choices and Decisions

Genesis 38:1-11

Beginning with Chapter 37, the remainder of Genesis focuses on the life of Joseph, except for Chapter 38. It seems odd and out of place. Yet, the story is significant as it gives insight into the man from whose lineage Jesus comes.

It is not the first time Judah is mentioned in Genesis, nor will it be the last. He was Jacob's fourth son, and for some unknown reason, he decided to leave his family. He went to Adullam. There, he met a man named Hirah, and they became friends. Adullam was a Canaanite city.[1] The Canaanite people did not believe in the God of Israel, and yet this is where Judah chose to go. He then married a Canaanite woman, and they had three sons.

Have you ever thought about those you are closest to and the influence they have on your life? If the majority of your friends are not Christian, yet this is who you choose to spend your time with, they will have an influence on you. There's nothing wrong about having friends who don't believe in Jesus, but if they are your closest associates, it's very possible they will lead you away from Him since He is not first in their lives.

When Judah's first son Er was old enough to marry, Judah chose a Canaanite woman named Tamar to be Er's wife. "But Er, Judah's firstborn, was wicked in the Lord's sight; so the Lord put him to death" (Genesis 38:7).

It was customary in those days for a widow to marry her deceased husband's brother to raise up an heir for the deceased.[2] Judah's second son, Onan, married Tamar. "Onan knew that the child would not be his; so whenever he slept with his brother's wife, he spilled his semen on the ground to keep from providing offspring for his brother. What he did was wicked in the Lord's sight; so the Lord put him to death also" (Genesis 38:9-10).

Imagine Judah's misery at losing two of his three sons. He'd given both of them to the same woman to marry, and they both died. Understandably, he might have had some apprehension about giving his remaining son to Tamar, and most likely had no intention of planning their marriage, though he didn't tell her that. Instead, "Judah then said to his daughter-in-law Tamar, 'Live as a widow in your father's household until my son Shelah grows up.' For he thought, 'He may die too, just like his brothers.' So Tamar went to live in her father's household" (Genesis 38:11).

More heartache and another deception, this time by Judah. Have you been deceived by someone you trusted? What was your first response when you realized it? Were you angry? Hurt? Revengeful? Though these are seemingly legitimate responses, wouldn't it be better to go to the Lord in prayer, and then wait for Him to help you?

Lord, I sometimes react too quickly when trials and heartache come my way. Rather than praying and waiting on You, I take matters into my own hands. Help me stop before acting on my own. Help me pray for Your direction, and then wait for Your answer. In Jesus' name, I pray. Amen.

Day 87

On the Road to Timnah

Genesis 38:12-23

After Judah's wife died and he recovered from his grief, he went with his friend Hirah to a sheering of the sheep in another town named Timnah. When Tamar received word of this, she quickly removed her widow's clothes. Twice deprived of a husband and children, and then realizing Shelah would not become her husband, she covered her face with a veil and sat down at the entrance to Enaim, which was on the road to Timnah.

In those days, women had little, if any, means of support outside of marriage. If their husband died without an heir, the wife was most likely relegated to a life of poverty. Tamar doesn't seem the type of woman to take that sitting down. She apparently wanted a family, even if it meant deception to get it.

Maybe she was hopeful Shelah would be with his father, but he wasn't. So she waited and tricked her father-in-law, who thought she was a prostitute and did not realize she was his daughter-in-law. "He went over to her by the roadside and said, 'Come now, let me sleep with you'" (Genesis 38:16).

Judah and Tamar had their tryst, and Tamar got what she went for. She procured Judah's seal, cord, and staff as collateral for the goat he promised to bring her. When Judah sent Hirah with the goat the next day to retrieve his items, the townspeople denied the existence of a prostitute on the road to Timnah. When Hirah told Judah, he dropped the matter. Even though he'd lost the items that identified him, he didn't want to pursue it further lest he became a laughingstock among the people. What others would think influenced him more than procuring what was rightfully his.

How often have we let what others think about us influence our decisions, especially when it comes to our relationship with Jesus? I've been intimidated by those who think my beliefs are whacky. I sometimes shy away from confrontation for fear of making someone else feel their opinion doesn't matter, even if I know what they are saying is wrong. I've found myself many times through the years apologizing to the Lord in prayer for not being more confident in who I am in Him. I know He changed my life, and I want everyone I love to have that same experience. But I often sit quietly when they ridicule my faith or use arguments to counter what I believe. I don't like to admit this because, after almost fifty years, I should know how to express what I believe. Instead, I do my best to live in a way that manifests His presence, praying my actions speak louder than my words.

Lord, it's hard not to be influenced by what others might think. Help me focus my attention on You when I'm faced with difficult decisions, for I truly want to honor You with my life. In Jesus' name, I pray. Amen.

Day 88

Day of Reckoning

Genesis 38:24-30

About three months later, unable to keep her pregnancy a secret, Tamar prepared for a confrontation. When Judah was told about her condition, he commanded, "Bring her out and have her burned to death!" (Genesis 38:24).

We should be careful what we say, or our words may come back to bite us. It did with Judah, for when Tamar was brought to her father-in-law, she sent a message to let him know who the father was. When he saw his seal, cord, and staff, there was no denying it. To his credit, he said, "She is more righteous than I, since I wouldn't give her to my son Shelah" (Genesis 38:26).

There is no mention of prayer by either Judah or Tamar before, during, or after these events. Tamar was a Canaanite, who did not know the God of Israel, and Judah certainly wasn't a good example of serving Him. If she did pray, it's not outlandish to think she prayed to the gods of Canaan such as Baal[1] and Molech[2].

Tamar was pregnant with twins. Little is said about their birth, except the one whose wrist was tied with a scarlet thread when he stuck his hand out first actually was born second. Sound familiar? Remember Esau and Jacob? Except their birthrights were exchanged much later, after their birth. Zerah, whose name means "scarlet" or "brightness," and had the scarlet thread on his wrist, came out second. Perez, whose name means "breaking out," somehow got in front of Zerah and came out first.

The first thing Matthew records in the New Testament is the genealogy of Jesus Christ. Who do we find in His lineage? Not only Judah and Perez, but Tamar; one of three women mentioned in Christ's genealogy. Tamar was a Canaanite, who did not serve the God of Israel; Ruth came from a culture of idol worship (Ruth

1:3-4); and Rahab was a prostitute (Joshua 2:1). These women were all Gentiles; yet, God used them in his plan of redemption.

With all our faults, the Creator of heaven and earth loves us so much He doesn't turn us away or leave us when we do wrong. He continually calls out to us, "Return to me and I will return you" (Zechariah 1:3 and Malachi 3:7). "If we confess our sins, he is faithful and just and will forgive us our sins and purify us from all unrighteousness" (1 John 1:9). He did it in the Old Testament, and also in the New.

Lord, thank You for giving the message in Your Word that You want me to come before You in my fallen condition, because this is the only way I can come to You. You give me explicit instructions on how to come out of that condition, by asking Jesus to forgive my sins. You also promise if I continue in my faith, established and firm, I am without blemish and free from accusation (Colossians 1:22-23). What a mighty, loving God You are. In Jesus' name, I pray. Amen.

Day 89

Potiphar's Wife

Genesis 39:1-23

Joseph's brothers had stripped him of his coat and stained it with goat's blood to trick their father into believing he was dead. But they couldn't strip Joseph of his virtue, and his faith. They separated Joseph from his father's house, but they couldn't separate Joseph from his God[1].

When Joseph arrived in Egypt with the caravan, he was sold to Potiphar, one of Pharaoh's officials and captain of the guard. Joseph is believed to have been a teenager at the time, but there is no indication he was fearful or full of self-pity. He apparently did what Potiphar commanded him to do (Colossians 3:22-24). It wasn't long before Potiphar realized Joseph was blessed by God and he put Joseph in charge of his entire household. This left Potiphar with nothing to concern himself about except what food to eat.

Joseph did not complain. He was obedient, taking each day and living it to its fullest. Though a slave, God's favor was on him, and he was rewarded mightily. He went about his duties in Potiphar's house until one day Potiphar's wife wanted to have sex with him. He refused and said he couldn't do such a wicked thing and sin against God (Genesis 39:7-9).

Scripture tells us to flee temptation, to not even let its desire take hold of us in our hearts (1 Corinthians 6:18 & 10:13, Matthew 5:27-28). Joseph knew this, and he refused to even be around Potiphar's wife.

"One day he went into the house to attend to his duties, and none of the household servants was inside. [Potiphar's wife] caught him by his cloak and said, 'Come to bed with me!' But he left his cloak in her hand and ran out of the house" (Genesis 39:11-13).

There is a very old saying, which I think applies in this case: "Hell hath no fury like a woman scorned."[2] Potiphar's wife was furious at being rejected by a slave. Once she realized she could use Joseph's cloak as evidence, she accused him of accosting her and making a fool of her and Potiphar.

Have you ever been wrongly accused? Most of us can probably think of a time or two. If or when this happens, we shouldn't seek or desire revenge, or it will consume us. "The Lord will fight for you; you need only be still" (Exodus 14:14).

We shouldn't "repay anyone evil for evil. Be careful to do what is right in the eyes of everyone. Do not take revenge, my dear friends, but leave room for God's wrath, for it is written, 'It is mine to avenge; I will repay,' says the Lord" (Romans 12:17, 19).

Did Potiphar believe his wife's story? He knew how faithful Joseph was and how he himself was blessed because of Joseph. As captain of the guard to Pharaoh, a very high position, he could have easily ordered Joseph's execution due to his wife's accusation. It seems he may have been doubtful about his wife's account because Potiphar instead sent Joseph to prison.

It wasn't long until Joseph's faithfulness to God was rewarded again. This time the warden put Joseph in charge of all those held in prison, giving him responsibility for all that was done there. The Lord gave Joseph favor in whatever he did.

Every time I read Joseph's story, it encourages me to know when things go awry, or nothing is going my way, God is there. I am reminded that God is always faithful (2 Timothy 2:13), and that in all things God works for the good of those who love Him, who have been called according to His purpose (Romans 8:28).

Let's not allow discouragement or depression to take hold when we know we've been wronged. Let's look to our heavenly Father. He sees our dilemma, and He will never leave nor forsake us (Hebrews 13:5). Like Joseph, we must remember to be patient.

Lord, thank You again for the life of Joseph. He endured so much. He was sold into slavery, wrongly accused, and forgotten. May his example encourage me to always look to You in my difficult times, in my worries, in my heartache, and in my pain. I ask for Your patience and endurance, especially during these times, trusting that You see, hear, and answer in Your perfect time. In Jesus' name, I pray. Amen.

Day 90

Not Forgotten

Genesis 40

Pharaoh's cupbearer and baker were in prison. They had been there for quite some time when Joseph noticed one day they were sad. He asked them, "Why do you look so sad today?" They both had dreams, and they were dejected because there was no one to interpret their dreams. Joseph said to them, "Do not interpretations belong to God? Tell me your dreams," and they did. After the cupbearer finished, Joseph interpreted his dream. Then the baker told Joseph his dream. Joseph interpreted it for him, even though it wasn't a good outcome (Genesis 40:4-19).

As a Christian, I am often inclined to tell others only about the goodness of God, but goodness is only one of His many attributes. He is also a just God, and He will one day judge the living and the dead (1 Peter 4:5).

Three days later, Joseph's interpretations came to pass. The baker was hanged and the cupbearer was restored to Pharaoh's palace. Before the cupbearer was released, Joseph asked, "When all goes well with you, remember me and show me kindness; mention me to Pharaoh and get me out of this prison" (Genesis 40:14). "The chief cupbearer, however, did not remember Joseph; he forgot him" (Genesis 40:23).

Matthew Cook, a pastor from Centerpoint Baptist Church, ended his sermon on Joseph with these words, "Joseph's fellow sufferers were like the two thieves that were crucified with Christ. One was saved, the other condemned. The one that was saved, however, forgot about Joseph and his plea in Genesis 40:14. Contrast that with Christ. When the dying thief asked to be remembered, Christ was faithful to do so in saying, 'Today you will be with Me in paradise!' Even though Joseph was forgotten by a man, he would never be forgotten by God."[1]

And God will never forget us, either (Isaiah 49:15).

No matter my circumstances, Lord, help me take solace in knowing that even when others forget me, You never will. In Jesus' name, I pray. Amen.

Day 91

Pharoah's Dream

Genesis 41:1-40

Joseph was enslaved and imprisoned for over twelve years, but his life was about to change drastically. Two full years after the cupbearer was restored to his position in the palace, he remembered Joseph after Pharoah had two dreams that troubled him greatly. When Pharoah's magicians and wise men were unable to interpret them, the cupbearer recounted his own experience with dreams. He explained that Joseph interpreted them and the interpretations came to pass exactly as he said.

I get excited when I read this story. It gives me hope and assurance, that God is faithful. Here was Joseph, perhaps wondering countless times, "When will God deliver me from these dingy, dark walls? I have done nothing to deserve this, yet here I am." Then, in one moment, he goes from prison to palace. He may not have realized at first what was taking place, but he would soon discover his patience, faithfulness, and prayers were answered.

"So Pharoah sent for Joseph, and he was quickly brought from the dungeon...Pharoah said to Joseph, 'I had a dream, and no one can interpret it. But I have heard it said of you that when you hear a dream you can interpret it.'

"'I cannot do it,' Joseph replied to Pharoah, 'but God will give Pharoah the answer he desires'" (Genesis 41:14-16).

Pharaoh told Joseph his dreams, and God gave Joseph the interpretation. Joseph made suggestions about how to prepare for the seven-year famine after seven years of plenty. Pharaoh realized there was no one better than Joseph to do the job, and he said to Joseph, "You shall be in charge of my palace, and all my people are to submit to your orders. Only with respect to the throne will I be greater than you" (Genesis 41:40).

Finally, after all these years of slavery and imprisonment, Joseph was not only free but given a position of authority over all of Pharaoh's people. Though he was now second in command in all of Egypt, Joseph never lost sight of God. He remained faithful, humble, loyal, and trustworthy. He knew God had a plan, and all of his misfortune was a part of it.

Have there been times in your life when you thought, "Things can't get any worse," and then they do? Have you ever gotten frustrated with God, even mad at him, or felt abandoned by Him? If so, read about Joseph as many times as it takes, until it sinks in that if anyone had reason to feel this way about God, Joseph did. Not once did he blame God for anything that happened to him. Not once did he take credit for being able to interpret dreams. Not once did he become resentful or prideful. By his actions, it's evident he always trusted God no matter what was happening to him.

God never forces us to serve Him. He gives us a choice, and when we choose Him, He will use us for His purposes. Joseph had no idea these events would take place. When they did, he was prepared because of all he went through. If we trust God when we are going through things we do not understand, He will do the same for us. We may not be second in command to a Pharaoh, but whatever God calls us to do will be for His glory.

Lord, thank You for the Bible that tells us Your whole story. Forgive me when things happen that I don't understand and I question You. Please give me a measure of faith so I will trust what You are doing, and, like Joseph, know everything will work out according to Your will. In Jesus' name, I pray. Amen.

Day 92

A New Name

Genesis 41:41-52

Other than Pharaoh, there was no one more powerful than Joseph throughout the land of Egypt. Pharaoh clothed Joseph in robes of fine linen, fastened a gold chain around his neck, and put a signet ring on his finger. This meant that any edict, order, document, or other element of society sealed with his ring carried Pharaoh's full authority.

Joseph didn't become egotistical or lazy in his new position. He believed Pharoah's dreams, and took his calling seriously. He traveled throughout Egypt, and prepared for the coming famine. For the next seven years, he collected and stored up huge quantities of grain, like the sand of the sea, from each of the Egyptian cities he visited.

Before the famine, Pharaoh gave Joseph the name Zaphenath-Paneah. Though there is no consensus as to its definition, one source says it may mean "revealer of secrets."[1] Whatever the meaning, it indicated Pharaoh was giving Joseph a new identity as an Egyptian noble[2], which also allowed him to be more easily integrated into Egyptian society.

Pharaoh then gave Joseph a wife named Asenath, daughter of Potiphera, priest of On. They had two sons. The firstborn was named Manasseh, meaning God made it possible for him to forget his trouble; and the second son was named Ephraim, meaning fruitful. God definitely brought Joseph out of his troubles, and made him fruitful.

There were other times in Genesis when God changed a person's name: Abram to Abraham; Sarai to Sarah; Jacob to Israel. Name changes signified not only that the old had passed away and a new time had begun, but it was an indication that the person's life would be completely altered from what it had previously been. It was almost like being born again.

In the New Testament, when Jesus met with Nicodemus, He spoke of being born again, not by natural birth but born of the Spirit (John 3:5-21). Jesus explained it this way, "Very truly, I tell you, no one can see the kingdom of God unless they are born again" (John 3:3). Though it is not a name change, it is comparable in the sense of being a new beginning. "Therefore, if anyone is in Christ, the new creation has come. The old has gone, the new is here!" (2 Corinthians 5:17).

In addition to that, Jesus said in Revelation 2:17, "To the one who is victorious... I will also give that person a white stone with a new name written on it, known only to the one who receives it."

Those in the Old Testament who received a new name from God meant their old way of life was finished and He had something completely new in store for them. Life for them would not be the same. And life is never the same for us when we receive Christ as our Savior.

We don't know yet what heaven will be like, but He who is seated on the throne said, "I am making everything new! Write this down, for these words are trustworthy and true" (Revelation 21:5).

Lord, thank You for Joseph's obedience to prepare for the day of famine so his family, Your chosen people, would be saved. Thank You also for sending Your Son Jesus to save me from my sins. It's exciting to read about those who came before me and how their lives were so transformed they received a new name. Thank you that you have also transformed my life through believing in Your Son Jesus as my Savior. I look forward to the day when I, too, will receive a new name and be with You forever in eternity. In Jesus' name, I pray. Amen.

Day 93

The Brothers Travel to Egypt

Genesis 41:53-57 & 42

By the time the seven years of famine began, Joseph was close to forty years old. He'd been second in command to Pharaoh for over seven years, gathering so much grain in all the cities of Egypt that it could not be counted. The people cried out to Pharaoh for food, and he told them, "Go to Joseph and do what he tells you." Joseph was prepared and began opening the storehouses to sell grain to the Egyptians (Genesis 41:55-56).

Sometimes I wonder if at this point Joseph was aware of his purpose for being in this high position. There's no indication he wavered in his faith or took advantage of others; he was going about the Lord's work preparing for what he knew was coming. Are we prepared, like Joseph, for whatever the Lord may have in store for us?

No, we are not all Josephs, and we won't all be second in command to a world leader, but God has a plan for each of us. When we go through difficult times, we need to seek Him diligently, drawing so close to Him that trust is not an issue. Like Joseph, the difficulties we go through may be the times that prepare us for what is ahead.

For Joseph, the pieces of the puzzle came together when his brothers arrived in Egypt. They had no idea who he was. They just knew they needed grain, and he was the one in charge. He spoke quite harshly to them, even accused them of being spies. They denied any wrong intentions, but Joseph put them in jail for three days anyway. Was this revenge for when they put Joseph in the cistern and left him begging for mercy?

Were his brothers contrite? Were they scared and worried about what was going to happen to them? Would you have been? There is not much doubt they were worried about their futures, and whether they were even going to survive. They had no idea the man to whom they just bowed down was their brother. But Joseph knew who they were, and he remembered his earlier dream as a young boy that they would one day bow down to him.

Was Joseph seeking the Lord's help and guidance about what to do? Was he coming to realize this was why he went through those tough times, so he could be in a position to help his family in their time of need?

After their three days in prison, Joseph ordered his brothers brought before him. He told them he feared God, and this was the deal: You can go back home with the grain, but one of your brothers has to stay behind. He chose Simeon and bound him before their eyes.

Joseph said further, "But you must bring your youngest brother to me, so that your words may be verified and that you may not die." They knew this request would be met with resistance from their father, but they had no choice. As they discussed their situation, not knowing Joseph understood them, they said to one another, "Surely we are being punished because of our brother [Joseph]. We saw how distressed he was when he pleaded with us for his life, but we would not listen; that's why this distress has come upon us." Joseph wept when he heard this (Genesis 42:20-24).

It had to have been difficult for Joseph to keep his identity hidden, but he longed to see his younger brother. I'm doubtful Joseph was taking revenge on his brothers, but by treating them harshly he was able to find out his father and younger brother were still alive. His harshness also resulted in his brothers coming to grips with what they had done to Joseph; hopefully making them feel guilty enough to ask God for forgiveness.

Before they left Egypt, Joseph ordered their bags to be filled with grain, along with the silver they brought to pay for it. Upon their return home, the brothers were frightened to discover the money hidden in the grain. Jacob was concerned as well. He lamented the loss of Joseph and now Simeon. He was adamant Benjamin would not go with his brothers when the time came to procure more grain.

Talk about family disunity. I imagine there was a lot of finger-pointing between their return home from Egypt and when they had to go back again for more grain.

Lord, these were tumultuous times for Joseph and his family. I don't know all the intricate details of what was going through their minds as these events unfolded, but I do know Your plan was being implemented. May I be like Joseph and trust that no matter how things seem to be going, You have everything under control. In Jesus' name, I pray. Amen.

Day 94

The Second Journey to Egypt

Genesis 43 & 44:13

Joseph's brothers must have been frightened at the thought of returning to Egypt. How would they explain the money found in their grain bags from their first visit? Their father finally agreed to let Benjamin go with them, but they didn't know what would happen to him, or them. They'd already lied to Jacob about Joseph being killed by a wild animal, and they knew he didn't want to lose Benjamin. It wasn't looking good for the brothers, but they knew they had to go or starve (Genesis 43:1-14).

Upon their arrival in Egypt, Joseph saw them come with Benjamin and told his steward to take them to his house and prepare a meal for them. This was very different from their first encounter with Joseph, and they were filled with fear. They tried explaining to Joseph's steward what happened with the silver, and how they came with double the money and gifts to show it was unintentional. Joseph's steward told them to look at it as a gift from God, and not to worry about it (Genesis 43:15-23).

To add to their fear and amazement, Joseph instructed his steward to seat his brothers at the table in their order of birth (Genesis 43:33). I don't know how they were coping, but I would have been looking for a way of escape. It was just too weird. But they had nowhere to go.

When Joseph came in, they were eager to present their gifts and bowed down before him to the ground. As a teenager, Joseph had two dreams this would happen one day, and this was the second time they bowed before him.

Joseph inquired about his father, Jacob, but when he was introduced to Benjamin, he couldn't contain himself. He left the room and went to his private chamber where he wept. He got control of himself, returned to his brothers, and ordered the food to be served. Benjamin received five times the amount of food as his brothers. Eyebrows must have lifted with curiosity as the hum of muffled whispers filled the air with questions of what exactly was happening to them. They soon relaxed and enjoyed a delightful feast (Genesis 43:27-34).

At dawn the next day, the brothers packed their donkeys, and left Egypt. Little did they know their good fortune was about to change when Joseph's steward chased after them, and accused them of stealing Joseph's silver cup. They adamantly denied doing such a thing. But there it was, hidden in the grain sack of Benjamin. Fear fell on these men, which caused them such great distress they tore their clothes (Genesis 44:3-13). This was an "expression of strong emotion such as shame, anger or mourning."[1]

Have you ever done something you regret so badly, you wish you could go back and change it? But that's impossible, isn't it? We only get one time around and don't have the privilege of erasing our past with a do-over. But when we do something wrong, if we don't make every effort to make it right, it will nag at us, perhaps even impinge on everything we think, do, and say.

All these years, Joseph's brothers lived with the guilt that they were the ones who sold their brother Joseph to be taken away. They had no idea where he was taken, or if he was even alive. They assumed what was happening to them was because of what they had done to Joseph.

Thank the Lord, because of Jesus it doesn't have to be that way for us any longer. "If we confess our sins, he is faithful and just and will forgive us our sins and purify us from all unrighteousness" (1 John 1:9). We don't have to live with the guilt caused by things we've done wrong. And if there is an opportunity to ask forgiveness of those we have wronged and sinned against, we are doubly blessed.

Lord, may I learn from the mistakes of others as I continue reading Your Word. Cause me to consider the consequences of my actions when I make decisions. Help me always to choose what honors and glorifies You. When I do sin against You and others, help me quickly repent and ask for forgiveness. In Jesus' name, I pray. Amen.

Day 95
Joseph's Identity Revealed

Genesis 44:14-45:24

Judah's desperate plea for Benjamin's freedom is in such stark contrast to when the brothers allowed Joseph to be sold, it's hard to believe he would fight so tenaciously. Judah pled for Benjamin's release. He explained to Joseph that their father would die if Benjamin did not return with them. Joseph was moved by the love shown toward Benjamin, and could no longer contain himself. He ordered his attendants to leave the room. Then he revealed himself to his brothers and began to weep uncontrollably (Genesis 44:14-45:2).

The atmosphere in that room must have been surreal; utter disbelief at what Joseph was saying. The more Joseph spoke, though, the more convinced his brothers became that yes, indeed, this was their little brother they had taken for dead. Can you even imagine their emotions: from disbelief to acceptance to excitement to all-out rejoicing? Instead of being solemn and sad, it became a party, and Benjamin received the longest hug from his big brother (Genesis 45:3-14).

It wasn't long until Pharaoh was told Joseph's brothers were in Egypt, and they were reunited for the first time in many years. Pharaoh was pleased and began pouring out blessing after blessing upon Joseph's brothers. He instructed them to return home, gather their families, and come back to Egypt, where they would be given the best land. Their good fortune continued when they were given carts and provision for the journey, as well as clothing, donkeys, grain, and bread. Joseph admonished them as they left Egypt. He must have seen their inclinations already, and he told them, "Don't quarrel on the way" (Genesis 45:16-24).

Would the outcome have been different if Joseph's brothers had the same callous attitude toward Benjamin as they did Joseph? Maybe, but we will never know.

What we can imagine is that throughout these more than twenty years, there were guilty whispers about what they had done to Joseph. This may have softened their attitudes toward each other, their father, and their youngest brother Benjamin, and made them realize the importance of sticking together as a family.

After Joseph revealed himself to his brothers, he told them, "And now, do not be distressed and do not be angry with yourselves for selling me here, because it was to save lives that God sent me ahead of you. But God sent me ahead of you to preserve for you a remnant on earth and to save your lives by a great deliverance" (Genesis 45:5 and 7). Joseph was fully aware of God's plan and purpose for his life, and the timing was perfect.

This isn't the only time Egypt was a place of refuge for God's people. In Matthew 2:13-15, an angel of the Lord appeared to Joseph (Mary's husband) in a dream and said, "Get up. Take the child and his mother and escape to Egypt. Stay there until I tell you, for Herod is going to search for the child to kill him." Joseph obeyed. They stayed in Egypt until Herod died, fulfilling what the Lord had said through the prophet, "Out of Egypt I called my son" (Hosea 11:1).

God does extraordinary things for His children when they obey. God had a plan for Joseph's life, and He knew how to fulfill it.

Sometimes we might wonder why God doesn't give the full picture of His plan for us. I believe the reason is we couldn't handle it if He did. I would be like Sarah who, in a hurry to fulfill God's plan, did it her own way. We've read how that worked out.

Let's relish the knowledge that when we believe in God, it is best to trust Him, especially when difficult times befall us.

Lord, I rejoice in the knowledge of Your plan to preserve Your people from starvation during a time of famine. May I be ever so diligent in trusting You when hard times come my way. In Jesus' name, I pray. Amen.

Day 96

The Journey from Canaan to Egypt

Genesis 45:25 to 46

Jacob must have been somewhat perplexed, or maybe overjoyed, when he saw his sons approaching. He could see they had grain and bread, but where had the carts and donkeys come from? The chatter and clatter of those returning to Canaan got louder and louder. In their excitement, they ran to their father, shouting, "Joseph is still alive! In fact, he is ruler of all Egypt" (Genesis 45:25-26).

"Have you lost your minds? What are you telling me?" Jacob may have responded in disbelief. His sons assured him they were telling the truth.

It's ironic that when his sons told him a lie, he believed it; now that they were telling him the truth, he didn't believe it.

Finally convinced, Jacob agreed to go, but not before stopping in Beersheba to offer sacrifices to the Lord. This is the same place Abraham and Isaac both called out to God, and it seems Jacob was not leaving there until he got answers to some questions, like: What about the land you promised me and my descendants? If we go to Egypt, is there a possibility my descendants will assimilate into Egyptian culture and refuse to return to Canaan? These were legitimate concerns considering the covenant God made with Abraham, Isaac, and Jacob. God assured Jacob in a dream that this was part of His plan, and that one day his descendants would surely return. For now, He wanted Jacob to be content knowing that Joseph's own hand would close his eyes (Genesis 46:1-4).

Off they went, seventy in all. That is not a very big group of people considering God promised that one day they would be as numerous as the stars in the sky and as the sand on the seashore (Genesis 22:17).

Jacob sent Judah to Joseph to get directions to Goshen, and Joseph wasted no time going to see his father. What a happy reunion as Joseph threw his arms around his father, and wept for a long time. Jacob was so content that he was ready to die right then (Genesis 46:28-30).

Joseph's relationship with the Lord was unsurpassed. His actions spoke more than a multitude of words ever could. There's no doubt Joseph saw the hand of God in this entire scenario, which culminated in a joyous reunion not only with his brothers but with his father, whom he loved.

As Christians, aren't we hoping and waiting for that great reunion that will one day bring everlasting joy? When we have fought the good fight, as Paul wrote to Timothy, when we have finished the race and kept the faith, we have no fear of death. For there is in store for us the crown of righteousness, which the Lord, the righteous Judge, will award us on that day, and not only us but also to all who have longed for His appearing (2 Timothy 4:6-8).

Lord, may I keep my eyes fixed on You, knowing when my days are over, I will see Jesus. There will be no more dying, only rejoicing in Your kingdom with You and all those who have gone before. In Jesus' name, I pray. Amen.

Day 97

Being Prepared

Genesis 47

Once his family settled in Goshen, the choicest land of Egypt, Joseph went about Pharaoh's business as the famine continued. He sold grain to the people until their money ran out. Then they sold their livestock to him in order to stay alive; then their land; and lastly, themselves, for they had no means to feed themselves other than the grain. Meanwhile, Jacob and his family prospered in Goshen (Genesis 47:13-27).

Today we don't have so much a food famine as we do a spiritual famine. God is excluded not only from our schools, but from anything having to do with government and the public domain, under the guise of separation of church and state. Yet, many of our founding documents clearly point to God. Now we find ourselves unprepared to deal with the crime, immorality, political corruption, and drug addiction that is happening in the lives of so many today.

It's never too late to make a change. Perhaps the fear that gripped our nation during the COVID-19 virus is a wake-up call to Christians everywhere. If you haven't been reading the Bible on a regular basis, start doing so today.

Paul wrote, "Be wise in the way you act toward outsiders; make the most of every opportunity. Let your conversation be always full of grace, seasoned with salt, so that you may know how to answer everyone" (Colossians 4:5-6). By knowing God's Word, we will be prepared to help those seeking answers to the problems we face.

Lord, help me listen when You tell me to prepare. I have been so busy doing other things to fill my time, I often neglect that which is most important, my time with You and the reading of Your Word. Forgive me, Father, and help me wake up to the realization that I am here for Your purposes. This is not my eternal home and I need to speak a word of encouragement and love to those whose hearts are crying out for help in a time of spiritual famine. In Jesus' name, I pray. Amen.

Day 98

Jacob and Two Grandsons

Genesis 48

Jacob's days were soon coming to an end. When Joseph got the news, he hurried with his two sons, Manasseh and Ephraim, to see his father. Jacob looked back over his life and spoke of the things most dear to him: God, Rachel, seeing Joseph again, and Joseph's sons (Genesis 48:1-7).

Let's pause for a moment and think about what it will be like when we are close to death. Lord willing, if we live to an old age and have time to be with family to consider what God did for us, it should be a somewhat happy occasion. The family ought to be able to look back and remember things that brought joy, comfort, and love. Then we should be prepared to go because of the knowledge Jesus gave us that "whoever hears my word and believes him who sent me has eternal life and will not be judged but has crossed over from death to life" (John 5:24).

Jacob had twelve sons and a daughter from his two wives and two concubines. He loved Rachel most, and getting to see Joseph and his grandchildren brought a double blessing, which Jacob then bestowed upon Manasseh and Ephraim, but not in their order of birth. Jacob was the younger son of Isaac, but he received the blessing of the eldest. Now Jacob conferred a blessing on the youngest of Joseph's sons. Joseph thought his father was making a mistake, and even tried taking his hand away from Ephraim's head. Jacob assured Joseph he knew what he was doing, and that the younger would be greater than the older (Genesis 48:12-20).

This was the fourth consecutive generation of Abraham's descendants in which the normal pattern of the firstborn assuming prominence over the secondborn was reversed: Isaac over Ishmael, Jacob over Esau, Joseph over Reuben, and Ephraim over Manasseh.[1]

Jacob adopted Joseph's sons, which made certain they would not stay behind in Egypt, and that their descendants would one day occupy the Promised Land. Joseph no longer objected to Jacob's blessings on his children.

This is the picture I want to have as death draws near: my children, grandchildren, and great-grandchildren at my bedside where we can share the goodness God bestowed on us. Then, I want to hand down the blessing of faith and be at peace knowing we will be together forevermore. "Praise be to the God and Father of our Lord Jesus Christ! In his great mercy he has given us new birth into a living hope through the resurrection of Jesus Christ from the dead, and into an inheritance that can never perish, spoil or fade. This inheritance is kept in heaven for you" (1 Peter 1:3-4).

Lord, those who came before paved the way for my own journey through life. When I read how they faltered, and You always lifted them up, it gives me hope that You will do the same for me. I am easily prone to putting You on the back burner of life when things are going my way. Help me remember I need You not only in the good times, but especially in the bad. May I remain faithful until my dying days, and may those whom I love do the same. In Jesus' name, I pray. Amen.

Day 99

Jacob's Blessings and Death

Genesis 49

Imagine the constant bickering and fighting over the years amongst twelve brothers, who all had the same father but came from four different mothers. Yet, God was with them. He brought them out of Canaan during a horrible famine, and now they were living in Goshen, the choicest land of Egypt.

Jacob enjoyed a few years of peace with his family. As is the fate of all of us, it came time for him to die, and he called for his sons. From the firstborn on down, he blessed his sons (sometimes sounding more like a curse), to include their descendants after them.

He began with Reuben, who slept with Bilhah, Rachel's maidservant. He paid dearly for his unstable ways by having his birthright stripped from him and his descendants. Simeon and Levi, who led the slaughter against Shechem after he raped their sister Dinah, were cursed for their anger and retribution, though their descendants were not totally stripped of their inheritance (Genesis 49:1-7).

When we do not trust the Lord's judgment for wrongdoings against us, we create more problems, not only for ourselves but for others. Had Simeon and Levi left the matter in God's hands, He would have dealt with it justly and fairly, and they would have had a clear conscience. It is best to remember the admonition "It is God who judges: He brings one down, he exalts another (Psalm 75:7).

Judah was chosen as the line from which the Messiah would come (Genesis 49:8-12). This is an interesting choice as he was the one who had sex with Tamar, his daughter-in-law, when he thought she was a prostitute. As we learned earlier from the book of Matthew, we find Perez, whose mother was Tamar, in the Messianic line (Matthew 1:1-3).

These people had many faults, none of which are hidden from us. Why is that? I believe it is so we can identify with them because we, too, have faults. We say and do things that are not always Christ-honoring. What a joy to know if we are "kind and compassionate to one another, forgiving each other, just as in Christ God forgave you," (Ephesians 4:32), we are indeed forgiven.

Continuing down the line are Zebulun, Issachar, Dan, Gad, Asher, and Naphtali. Their significance is not diminished because they are not as prominent in the events of history. We don't know as much about these sons as we do the others, but they and their descendants are among the twelve tribes of Israel mentioned throughout the Old and New Testaments (Genesis 49:13-21).

Then there is Joseph, the one man who stands out above all others in Genesis. He is a type of Christ in many ways. Joseph was persecuted, and hated by his own brothers who sold him into slavery. Jesus was mocked and continually ridiculed by those who did not believe He was the Messiah (Luke 22:63). He was betrayed for thirty pieces of silver by one of His disciples (Matthew 26:15).

There is not one hint of unrighteousness, unfaithfulness or distrust about Joseph. No matter his predicament, he never said one harsh word about another person; nor did he blame anything or anyone for his undeserved slavery and imprisonment. He was silent. Jesus, too, was silent as he stood before his accusers (Mark 14:61).

Though Joseph did not die for our sins, he was taken from the jail in which he was imprisoned and given the most prominent position in Egypt, second in command to Pharaoh. This made it possible to save his entire family from the famine. Jesus was falsely accused, mistreated, and then hung on a cross to die. He spent three days in a tomb, and on the third day rose again. Victorious over death, he ascended into heaven where He is now seated at the right hand of God (Romans 8:34).

Christianity is not some rigid form of religion. It is a real and intimate relationship with a person. That person is Jesus Christ, the Son of God. May our hearts be thankful to those who came before us, the ones who paved the way for the most significant event in this world: the birth, life, death, and resurrection of our Savior!

Holy Spirit, I call upon You to help me with my weaknesses and hardships. May I always to be mindful of Your presence, and not forget the hope to which I am called. Help me remember my struggle is not against flesh and blood, but against the rulers, against the authorities, against the powers of this dark world and against the spiritual forces of evil in the heavenly realms (Ephesians 6:11-12). In Jesus' name, I pray. Amen.

Day 100
Deaths of Jacob and Joseph

Genesis 50

Joseph was full of sorrow, threw himself onto Jacob's dead body, and wept. I know what it's like to lose your dad, and it is a sorrowful time. One of the people responsible for bringing you into this world is gone, and life will be different from now on.

Jacob's one request to Joseph was after he died he wanted to be buried in the land of Canaan where his father and grandfather were buried. Joseph explained the situation to Pharaoh, who honored Joseph's request, and sent some of his own people to accompany Joseph and his family (Genesis 50:4-8). Pharaoh was so grateful to Joseph, he denied him nothing when he asked.

Jacob's body was returned to the land of Canaan, and buried in the cave in the field of Machpelah, near Mamre, which Abraham bought as a burial place. Jacob was buried next to Abraham, Isaac, and his wife Leah. After the burial, Joseph, his brothers, and all who went with them returned to Egypt (Genesis 50:12-14). Burying a loved one is always difficult.

His brothers still carried guilt about what they had done to Joseph, and were fearful Joseph would punish them now that their father was dead. They sent word to Joseph, "Your father left these instructions before he died: 'This is what you are to say to Joseph: I ask you to forgive your brothers the sins and wrongs they committed in treating you so badly.' Now please forgive the sins of the servants of the God of your father." When Joseph received this message, he wept (Genesis 50:16-17). We don't know why he wept. Perhaps he was hurt that his brothers still thought he would take revenge on them for what they did so many years earlier.

Joseph, in his tender and mild way of saying things, assured his brothers they shouldn't be afraid, but said to remember, "You intended to harm me, but God intended it for good to accomplish what is now being done, the saving of many lives. So then, don't be afraid. I will provide for you and your children" (Genesis 50:20-21).

Some of us go through much more difficult and trying times than others, and it may even seem unbearable to endure. As Christ-followers, we are told to "trust in the Lord with all your heart and lean not on our own understanding; in all our ways submit to him, and he will make your paths straight" (Proverbs 3:5-6). Joseph did, and look what happened to him.

Joseph died at the age of one hundred ten. "Then Joseph said to his brothers, 'I am about to die. But God will surely come to your aid and take you up out of this land to the land he promised on oath to Abraham, Isaac and Jacob.' And Joseph made the Israelites swear an oath and said, 'God will surely come to your aid, and then you must carry my bones up from this place'" (Genesis 50:24-25).

Little did he know it would be four hundred years until this would occur. "And Joseph's bones, which the Israelites had brought up from Egypt, were buried at Shechem in the tract of land that Jacob bought for a hundred pieces of silver from the sons of Hamor, the father of Shechem. This became the inheritance of Joseph's descendants" (Joshua 24:32).

Lord, whatever my sorrow, whatever my pain, keep me always mindful that what someone else intends for evil, You, O Lord, intend for good. As I reflect upon the lives of Jacob and Joseph, may I be reminded of Your unfailing love. May my heart be filled to overflowing with the knowledge that You are Almighty God, the Creator of all things, and that my destiny is in Your hands. In Jesus' name, I pray. Amen.

Afterword

It's been a long journey through the book of Genesis. I pray you have been strengthened in faith, and blessed in spirit. As we conclude, take some time to ponder these questions:

Why is it important to believe sin originated in the Garden of Eden?

How does the decision of Adam and Eve to disobey God affect our lives today?

What has helped you better understand that you are important to God, the Creator of heaven and earth?

How has God shown you that you are on earth at this time because this is where He intended for you to be?

What connection, if any, do you believe you have to those who blazed the path before us, who were part of making the way for the Messiah to come so we could be reunited with our heavenly Father after sin entered into the world?

Do you believe that even before God created the world, He had a plan for salvation through Jesus Christ that would bring you into an intimate relationship with Him? If not, what is preventing you from believing this today?

If some of these questions are difficult to answer, is it possible there are unresolved wounds that need to be dealt with openly and honestly?

The best way I know to open up to God, to Jesus, to the Holy Spirit, is to humble myself by getting on my knees and asking forgiveness so my brokenness can be healed. He has set me free (more than once!) so I can be the person He made me to be. He wants me, and you, to live our lives to the fullest, and honor Him while doing so.

He has given us the tools to do it. It began in Genesis and continues through to the end of Revelation, where we know how the story ends. For those who believe in the Lord Jesus Christ as the Son of God, the Savior of the world, the Redeemer of Israel—the One who died on a cross, was buried, rose again, and is seated at the right hand of God—the war has been won. The victory is ours for all of eternity! That is a glorious promise. It is something to shout about, and praise the Lord for.

The book of Revelation offers some of the most reassuring words of our Lord Jesus Christ. He said,

Look, I am coming soon! My reward is with me, and I will give to each person according to what they have done. I am the Alpha and the Omega, the First and the Last, the Beginning and the End. Blessed are those who wash their robes, that they may have the right to the tree of life and may go through the gates into the city. Outside are the dogs, those who practice magic arts, the sexually immoral, the murderers, the idolaters and everyone who loves and practices falsehood. I, Jesus, have sent my angel to give you this testimony for the churches. I am the Root and the Offspring of David, the bright Morning Star. Yes, I am coming soon (Revelation 22:12-16, 20).

And I heard a loud voice from the throne say, "Look! God's dwelling place is now among the people, and he will dwell with them. They will be his people, and God himself will be with them and be their God. He will wipe every tear from their eyes. There will be no more death or mourning or crying or pain, for the old order of things has passed away" (Revelation 21:3-4).

Everything that happened in Genesis forged a path toward this very end. I believe those we came to know and love in the first book of the Bible will be in heaven waiting to greet us. And we will be together forevermore.

Prayer of Faith

If you have not made a commitment to follow Christ as your Savior but would like to, ask Him now to forgive your sins, to come into your heart and fill you with the Holy Spirit. Ask Him to give you a desire and willingness to follow Him from this day forward. It is a new beginning, one that will take you into eternity. Begin reading your Bible and praying. Find a church that teaches and believes in the inerrancy of God's Word. Join a small group Bible study. This is a life-long journey that is not meant to be traveled alone!

Thank you for allowing me to walk you through the wonderful book of Genesis, where God spoke and time began.

God bless.

About the Author

After working as a court reporter in the federal court system for fifteen years, Mindi worked ten years on Capitol Hill as an Official Reporter of Debates for both the House and Senate. She retired in 2006, and moved to Florida. In August 2013, her life changed dramatically when a mutual friend introduced her to Tom, whose first wife passed away in 2011. They were a perfect fit for each other. He was a widower, and she had never been married. In November of 2023, they celebrated their tenth anniversary. They live in Murfreesboro, Tennessee, and are blessed with two children, three grandchildren, and four great-grandchildren. They love to travel and entertain, as well as volunteer at church.

Mindi has loved words all her life. She began writing letters to friends and family at a young age. During her career, she wrote articles for both the United States Court Reporters Association and the National Court Reporters Association. As a court reporter, she wrote down thousands of words of the famous and not so famous. Since retiring, her love of words hasn't stopped. She's written many unpublished short stories about her travels to parts of Europe, and around the United States, honing her skills of description to bring readers to places they might never visit. One day, maybe she'll publish those stories.

Her love for Jesus, combined with her love of words, gave her inspiration to write *Your True Origin Story*. If time permits, in the future she may write additional devotionals on other books of the Old Testament.

For more information or to connect with Mindi, visit her at papercrownmedia.com/mindi.

Endnotes

Day 1

1. Youtube.com/watch?v+Y3lp0z981iM (beginning at time marker 7:23)

Day 3

1. https://www.bibleplaces.com/cedar-of-lebanon/

2. https://answersingenesis.org/geology/natural-features/niagara-falls-and-the-bible/

3. https://www.youtube.com/watch?v=5uYzQQug2-o

Day 5

1. https://www.sciencenews.org/article/5000-deep-sea-animals-new-ocean

Day 7

1. https://answersingenesis.org/bible-characters/moses/did-moses-write-genesis/

2. Exodus 17:14, 24:4, 34:27; Numbers 33:1-2; Joshua 1:8, 8:31-32, 23:6; 1 Kings 2:3; 2 Kings 14:6; Ezra 6:18; Nehemiah 13:1, Daniel 9:11-13; Malachi 4:4; Matthew 8:4, 19:8, Mark 12:26; Luke 24:27, 24:44; John 5:45-47; Acts 3:22; Romans 10:5, 1 Corinthians 9:9; 2 Corinthians 3:15

3. https://bible.org/article/introduction-pentateuch

Day 18

1. https://www.dailysignal.com/2021/07/16/inconvenient-truth-no-one-actually-changes-gender-only-ones-persona/

2. https://www.nbcnews.com/feature/nbc-out/boy-or-girl-parents-raising-theybies-let-kids-decide-n891836

3. https://humanevents.com/2023/11/05/savanah-hernandez-father-faces-restraining-order-for-not-affirming-5-year-old-sons-trans-identity

Day 19

1. https://answersingenesis.org/bible-timeline/genealogy/when-did-methuselah-die/

2. https://idioms.thefreedictionary.com/as+old+as+Methuselah

Day 20

1. https://arkencounter.com/

Day 23

1. Dennis Prager, Genesis, God, Creation and Destruction, Page 129

2. The NIV Matthew Henry Commentary in One Volume, Page 24

Day 27

1. https://biblehub.com/hebrew/5674.htm

2. http://www.quora.com/What-does-Eber-mean-in-Hebrew
   https://www.ancient-hebrew.org/names/Eber.htm

Day 28

1. https://www.ethnologue.com/guides/how-many-languages

2. *Discovering the Old Testament, Story and Faith* by Alex Varughese, Editor; Robert D. Branson, Jim Edlin and Tim M. Green, page 73

Day 37

1. Webster's International Dictionary of the English Language,

   Second Edition, Unabridged, 1936

Day 40

1. https://www.biblegateway.com/resources/encyclopedia-of-the-bible/Pseudepigrapha

2. https://www.bereanbiblechurch.org/transcripts/galatians/gal_04_21-31_these-women-are-two-covenants.htm

Day 42

1. https://www.biblegateway.com/resources/encyclopedia-of-the-bible/Beer-Lahai-Roi-Beer-La-Hai-Roi

2. https://www.christianity.com/wiki/people/why-did-god-bless-ishmael.html

Day 43

1. https://www.christianwebsite.com/what-does-isaac-mean-in-the-bible/

Day 45

1. https://www.biblicalarchaeology.org/daily/biblical-sites-places/biblical-archaeology-sites/where-is-sodom/ , https://bibleatlas.org/sodom_and_gomorrah.htm

Day 47

1. https://biblehub.com/commentaries/isaiah/15-1.htm

2. https://uasvbible.org/2024/02/18/the-ammonites-descendants-of-lot-and-adversaries-of-israel-in-the-biblical-narrative/

Day 51

1. Pawson, David. Sermon Old Testament Studies: Genesis 21 https://www.davidpawson.org/resources/resource/761?return_url=https%3A%2F%2Fwww.davidpawson.org%2Fresources%2Fcategory%2Fold-testament-studies%2Fgenesis%2F

Day 52

1. http://www.biblestudytools.com/dictionary/beersheba

Day 55

1. The NIV Matthew Henry Commentary in One Volume, 1992, page 43

2. https://www.thetorah.com/article/abraham-negotiates-to-buy-the-cave-of-the-machpelah-in-the-promised-land

Day 56

1. Prager, Dennis *Genesis, God, Creation and Destruction* Chapter 24, page 270 (24.2); https://www.gotquestions.org/hand-under-thigh.html

2. https://biblehub.com/commentaries/genesis/24-2.htm

Day 60

1. Pawson, David. Sermon Old Testament Studies: Genesis 24 https://www.davidpawson.org/resources/resource/758?return_url=https%3A%2F%2Fwww.davidpawson.org%2Fresources%2Fcategory%2Fold-testament-studies%2Fgenesis%2F

Day 61

1. https://en.wikipedia.org/wiki/Ishmael

Day 63

1. https://biblehub.com/sermons/auth/armstrong/godly_and_worldly_sorrow.htm

2. https://inspiredscripture.com/bible-studies/genesis-35#gsc.tab=0

Day 67

1. Deffinbaugh, Robert. May 12.2004. "From Paradise to Patriarchs, Working Like the Devil Serving the Lord." https://bible.org/seriespage/28-working-devil-serving-lord-genesis-271-46

Day 68

1. https://biblicaldefinitions.com/exploring-bethel-in-the-bible-spiritual-significance/

2. https://www.biblestudytools.com/dictionary/luz/

Day 70

1. Hobson, Tom. October 12, 2017. "What was Wrong with Leah's Eyes?" https://www.patheos.com/blogs/tomhobson/2017/10/wrong-leahs-eyes/

Day 74

1. https://www.bibleodyssey.org/articles/household-gods/

2. https://www.blueletterbible.org/esv-study-bible/old-testament/facts/genesis-fact-24.cfm

Day 76

1. https://www.biblegateway.com/resources/encyclopedia-of-the-bible/Mahanaim

Day 77

1. Henry, Matthew. *The NIV Matthew Henry Commentary in One Volume*, 1992, page 55, verses 9-12. "Times of fear should be times of prayer; whatever frightens us should drive us to our knees, to our God."

Day 80

1. https://www.biblegateway.com/resources/encyclopedia-of-the-bible/El-Elohe-Israel

2. https://www.chabad.org/library/article_cdo/aid/2153/jewish/What-is-the-Torah.htm

3. Prager, Dennis. Genesis, God, Creation, and Destruction, page 404

Day 82

1. https://www.christianity.com/church/church-history/timeline/1-300/whatever-happened-to-the-twelve-apostles-11629558.html

Day 83

1. https://www.compellingtruth.org/Edomites.html

Day 86

1. https://www.biblegateway.com/resources/encyclopedia-of-the-bible/Adullam

2. *NIV Cultural Backgrounds Study Bible*, page 85, Levirate Marriage

Day 88

1. https://www.gotquestions.org/who-Baal.html

2. https://theologyinfive.com/molech-a-deity-of-ancient-canaanite-religion-as-referenced-in-the-bible/

Day 89

1. Henry, Matthew. *Matthew Henry's Commentary on the Whole Bible (Complete)*. Vol. I. M.p. 1706. Page 62 https://www.biblestudytools.com/commentaries/matthew-henry-complete/genesis/38.html

2. https://nosweatshakespeare.com/quotes/famous/hell-hath-no-fury-like-a-woman-scorned/

Day 90

1. Cook, Matthew, Feb 24, 2005, "The Cupbearer & The Baker," Sermon. https://www.sermoncentral.com/sermons/the-cupbearer-the-baker-matthew-cook-sermon-on-god-s-omniscience-76727?page=2&wc=800

Day 92

1. https://bibletruthpublishers.com/zaphnath-paaneah/ljm16847

2. *NIV Cultural Backgrounds Study Bible*, page 91, footnote 41:45

Day 94

1. Oladokum, Sarah. June 8, 2017. "Why did People in the Old Testament Tear Their Robes?" https://www.christiantoday.com/article/why-did-people-in-the-old-testament-tear-their-robes/109889.htm

Day 98

1. Cole, Steven. https://www.bibleoutlines.com/genesis-481-22-crossed-hands-of-blessing-putting-ephraim-before-manasseh/

www.ingramcontent.com/pod-product-compliance
Lightning Source LLC
Chambersburg PA
CBHW071312110426
42743CB00042B/1285